Lucid dreaming

Since Celia Green wrote her original study of lucid dreaming in 1968, interest in the field has spread and new research findings have been generated. *Lucid Dreaming* is both a review of these developments and a new contribution to the theoretical interpretation of the subject.

Three main areas are covered: the phenomenology of lucid dreams (what it is like to be asleep and dreaming and to realise that you are doing so); the relationship between lucid dreams and other hallucinatory states; and the practical applications of lucid dreaming.

Containing much fascinating first-hand case material, *Lucid Dreaming* illustrates how lucid dreams may be developed, and how the dreamer may acquire a degree of control over them.

Celia Green is the Director of the Institute of Psychophysical Research, Oxford, and is the author of several books, including *Lucid Dreams* (1968) and *The Human Evasion* (1969). **Charles McCreery** is Research Officer at the Institute of Psychophysical Research. He received a doctorate from Oxford University for work on the psychology and physiology of out-of-the-body experiences. His previous books include *Psychical Phenomena and the Physical World* (1973).

Lucid dreaming

The paradox of consciousness during sleep

Celia Green and Charles McCreery

Routledge
Taylor & Francis Group

LONDON AND NEW YORK

First published 1994
by Routledge
27 Church Road, Hove, East Sussex BN3 2FA

Simultaneously published in the USA and Canada
by Routledge
711 Third Avenue, New York, NY 10017

Reprinted 1999, 2001 and 2007

Transferred to Digital Printing 2011

Routledge is an imprint of the Taylor & Francis Group, an Informa business

© 1994 Institute of Psychophysical Research

Typeset in Palatino by LaserScript, Mitcham, Surrey

British Library Cataloguing in Publication Data
A catalogue record for this book is available from the British Library

Library of Congress Cataloging in Publication Data
A catalog record for this book has been requested

ISBN 978-0-415-11239-0 (pbk)

Publisher's Note
The publisher has gone to great lengths to ensure the quality of this reprint
but points out that some imperfections in the original may be apparent.

Contents

Figure and tables

FIGURE

TABLES

Introduction and acknowledgements

The purpose of this book is twofold: first, to provide a general introduction to the topic of lucid dreaming (dreams in which the subject is aware that he or she is dreaming); and secondly, to propose a new theoretical framework for the phenomenon. The book is intended both for specialist professionals, such as psychologists and philosophers, to whose fields of interest the subject is particularly relevant, and for the general reader with an interest in the topic. For the purposes of the latter group we have aimed at clarity in general, and in particular have attempted to explain any technical terms as we go along. For the purposes of the former group we have attempted to reference any assertions and generalisations as fully as possible, and in particular to direct the reader to other publications where a specific topic has been dealt with more fully elsewhere.

We believe the phenomenon of lucid dreaming is of interest and importance for three main reasons. First, because of the intrinsic interest of the state itself, a 'paradoxical' state of consciousness, apparently intermediate between non-lucid sleep and wakefulness. Secondly, because of its relations with other hallucinatory states reported by normal people, such as 'out-of-the-body' experiences and apparitions. And thirdly, because of its potential practical applications, particularly in the treatment of nightmares, for example in children and people suffering from post-traumatic stress disorder.

The arrangement of the book follows this threefold division to some extent. Some of the earlier chapters (e.g. Chapters 3, 4 and 5) are mainly about the phenomenology of lucid dreaming (what it is like to be asleep and to know that one is asleep and dreaming); Chapters 6, 7 and 8 discuss the relationship of lucid dreams to other hallucinatory experiences, and present a theoretical framework for hallucinatory experiences in general; and Chapters 9 to 14 deal more with the possible practical applications and effects of lucid dreaming, including the questions of induction and control. The final chapter contains some neurophysiological hypotheses, both about the accompaniments of the state itself and the individual differences of neural organisation which may predispose people to experience it.

The book is intended to complement rather than supersede Celia Green's book *Lucid Dreams*, first published in 1968. We have deliberately avoided re-using case material from the earlier book, except in a few instances where it was unavoidable, and instead have drawn on the considerable quantity of case material which has accumulated since 1968, both in our own collection and in published sources. There is inevitably some overlap of subject matter, as we wished the new book to be self-sufficient, i.e. to be an adequate introduction to the subject for people who had not read the earlier book. However, we felt there was a place for a general survey of the present kind in view of the research findings that have been made since the publication of the earlier book, and in the light of the various theoretical ideas which we will be putting forward.

We should like to record our indebtedness to our colleagues in the writing of this book: Christine Fulcher, for help with word-processing; William Leslie, for research on case material; and Fabian Tassano, for reading the entire book twice, and making numerous suggestions, both large and small, for its improvement.

We should also like to thank the following for providing us with information of various kinds: Dr Jayne Gackenbach, Dr George Gillespie, Dr Keith Hearne, Dr Harry Hunt, Dr Stephen LaBerge, Professor Paul Tholey, and Alan Worsley.

The following have kindly agreed to allow us to quote from copyright material: Dr John Cutting, Dr Ann Faraday, Dr Patricia Garfield, Dr Kenneth Kelzer, Dr Stephen LaBerge, Dr Alfred Lischka, B. G. Marcot, Oxford University Press, Professor Elaine Pagels, Professor Oliver Sacks, the American Society for Psychical Research, Professor Paul Tholey, and Professor J. H. M. Whiteman. Full references will be found in the text and bibliography.

We are grateful to Dr Gordon Claridge for reading several chapters and making a number of very helpful suggestions.

Finally, we should like to thank all our subjects, who have helped over the years without any financial reward.

Chapter 1

Definition, illustrations and historical background

DEFINITION AND ILLUSTRATIVE EXAMPLES

Lucid dreams are those in which a person becomes aware that he is dreaming. As he realises this the character of the dream changes, and as long as he remains aware of his state, he continues to be in a lucid dream. A lucid dream differs in many respects from an ordinary dream; it may be extremely realistic and provide the dreamer with a strikingly convincing imitation of waking life, and its emotional tone is often positive, sometimes to the point of elation.

The following lucid dream, reported by Oliver Fox, the author of a book about his own lucid dreams and out-of-the-body experiences,[1] illustrates some of the characteristic features of lucid dreams. It will be seen that Fox reports what appears to be a relatively high level of cognitive functioning, with insight into his condition and memory of the basic facts of his life, including the position of his physical body.

> I dreamed that I was walking, by day, through some un-familiar street containing very fine buildings. There were plenty of people about in ordinary attire. Some incident or incongruous detail, which I cannot remember, told me I was dreaming, and I decided to experiment in prolonging the dream. I just walked on, like a visitor to a strange town. I noticed that I was dressed in the uniform of an army officer; so when I passed a very fine War Memorial, I played my part by giving it 'eyes left' and saluting. I also returned the salute of a soldier who happened to pass me. The uniform was brown, but I am not sure whether it was British. Nevertheless I had perfect consciousness of my real physical condition. I knew I

was a Clerical Officer at the —— Dept. and that my body was at home in Worple Road. I knew also that in my army days I was only a private.

By and by I left the street and found myself on a pretty country road. The hedgerows and trees were in full leaf, and the sky blue and sunlit. I had my usual feeling (in these experiments) of wonderful health and vitality, and the atmosphere was charged with beauty and the sense of coming adventure.

(Fox, 1962, pp. 111–12)

Lucid dreams have only recently gained recognition as a phenomenon which has to be considered separately from ordinary dreaming, and it is only in the last fifteen years or so that they have started to be the subject of research by psychologists and physiologists. It seems a strange phenomenon in itself that they should have remained almost unrecognised for so long, since they seem to be fairly easy for people to learn to have, and are usually valued as an interesting experience by those who have them.

Lucid dreams appear to be accessible to a fair proportion of the population, and a great many people experience them spontaneously at some stage of their lives. There is also a small number of individuals who experience lucid dreams regularly. It appears to be rare, however, for a person to become a habitual lucid dreamer without some deliberate intention to cultivate them. On the other hand, people who have never had them before (as far as they remember) may find that reading a book about them and applying some analytical thought to their possibilities is sufficient for them to start dreaming in this way.

The following dream is from one of our subjects who came to have lucid dreams as a result of reading about them. It illustrates the positive emotions which may be experienced in lucid dreams, though not all lucid dreamers report such a high degree of elation.

I was in a strange country-style kitchen, sitting at the table and looking at the notepaper which I had bought yesterday in real life. As I opened the box, I noticed that instead of blank stationery, it contained already sealed and addressed envelopes (the first was for a friend in America). I thought, 'but that's not possible, I only bought these today and I know they were blank then.' Then suddenly light dawns and I think 'BUT

THIS MUST BE A DREAM THEN!' I am elated at finally understanding why things are so ridiculous, and my overall feeling is of being tremendously happy at this release from worrying about the illogic around me. I start to rise up after this realisation comes and I fly towards the window. I go out 'swimming' through the air, having decided to see if breast stroke is possible in thin air. As I fly, I can remember all my intentions about lucid dream experimentation. I laugh at my scepticism at how exhilarating flying dreams could be. The most important thing is that throughout I am in control.

(Subject S. R.)

In her earlier study of the present topic, Green (1968a) adopted the term 'lucid dream', which was used by van Eeden (1913) to designate dreams in which he knew he was dreaming, in preference to the names given by some other lucid dreamers, such as Oliver Fox, who called them 'dreams of knowledge'. This terminology has now been generally adopted. We think it is important to restrict the definition of a lucid dream entirely to the presence or absence of this one factor, the dreamer's awareness of his state.

Because dreams in which a person knows he or she is dreaming tend, as a group, to have other characteristic features which distinguish them from ordinary dreams, and also because they are in the literal sense of the word 'lucid', in that the dreamer seems to be rational and clear-headed, it has sometimes been suggested that the definition of a lucid dream should be made to depend on some composite of these other qualities. For example, it has been suggested that a dream should be regarded as lucid only if, in addition to the dreamer's preserving awareness that he is dreaming, he also has complete memory of his waking life and a high level of control of the developments within the dream (Tart, 1988).

This proposal, however, seems to us unsatisfactory in a number of ways. First, it would shift the basis of classification from a simple all-or-none factor to something which has to be subjectively assessed on some kind of sliding scale. Secondly, it is not a realistic proposal that a lucid dreamer should assess whether, or to what extent, he really has access to his full range of waking memories, or to what extent he is able to influence the dream events. He may have a strong sense that he is particularly 'all there' in a certain dream, and might therefore be tempted to classify it as 'more lucid' than one in which he feels this less strongly, but it is actually only by experiment within the dream that it is possible to discover restrictions which may actually be present upon his ability to recall his normal life or his control of the dream, and there is no scope within any given dream for more than a limited number of experiments bearing upon these points.

It seems to us more satisfactory to retain the original definition of a lucid dream as depending on one factor only. This, of course, leaves the way open for research into the extent to which this factor is found in combination with different degrees of memory and intellectual functioning.

HISTORICAL DEVELOPMENT

It may be helpful to characterise the status of lucid dream reports at the time of the first author's book *Lucid Dreams*. Certain individuals had reported that they occasionally had dreams in which they were aware of their situation and were able to remember and reason in a normal way. But were they really doing this, or were they only dreaming about doing it? The idea of lucid dreaming aroused resistance in various quarters because dreams were felt to be an essentially irrational state, and some philosophers took refuge in the suggestion that lucid dreams were merely a variant on the common dream feature of 'dreaming that x', where x in this case equated with 'one is dreaming' rather than, say, 'one is flying'. Lucid dreamers were not, it was sometimes suggested to us, aware that they were dreaming, but dreaming that they were aware.

The resistance to the idea of lucid dreaming was associated, for some people, with a generalised deprecation of the dream state. Rationality, according to this mode of thought, is inseparable from the reality in which it functions, and in particular with the waking state in which communication with others takes place. Some philosophers, such as Malcolm (1959), went so far as seemingly to doubt that a dream ever happened (that, at least, is the message which Malcolm's book *Dreaming* suggests, even if Malcolm himself never explicitly admits that this is the implication of his arguments). According to Macolm, the 'real' world is that in which people communicate with one another and confirm one another's observations. In this world, all that verifiably takes

place is that people sometimes feel inclined on waking to narrate
a sequence of experiences which they say they have just had.
Alternatively, some psychologists, such as Hartmann (1975),
suggested that reports of lucid dreams were really reports of brief
periods of wakefulness, or 'brief partial arousals', and hence
closer to daydreams than to a true dream. This is a proposal
which would probably only seem plausible to someone who had
never experienced lucidity in the dream state. It seems to us that
anyone who had ever become lucid during a dream would
consider it inapplicable, if only because he would know that one
remains fully immersed in the perceptual world of the dream,
and does not suddenly become aware instead, or as well, of the
real world or any part of it, such as the feel of the bed in which
one is lying. This point will be illustrated by several examples
later in this book, in which it is clear that lucid dreamers may be
quite uncertain of the location of their physical body while they
are lucid. For example, on page 107 we quote a case in which a
lucid dreamer, who is dreaming of being at his desk in a chair,
wonders if his physical body is in that position in reality (in fact
he is lying in bed in the normal way). Indeed it seems to be
particularly difficult for some lucid dreamers to recall the
immediate circumstances of their waking life, such as where they
went to sleep the night before.

The fact that scepticism about the possibility of lucidity in
dreams may be linked to the fact of a person's never having
experienced it is illustrated by the following passage by a writer
on dreams from the early years of this century, Havelock Ellis. It
will be seen that the statement of his sceptical position
immediately follows his admission that he himself has never
experienced lucidity. It is also interesting to note that he
produced what is essentially the same hypothesis as Hartmann to
explain those statements he knew of by other writers that they
have indeed at times been lucid while dreaming.

I have never detected in my own dreams any recognition that
they are dreams. I may say, indeed, that I do not consider that
such a thing is really possible, although it has been borne
witness to by many philosophers and others from Aristotle
and Synesius and Gassendi onwards. The phenomenon
occurs; the person who says to himself that he is dreaming
believes that he is still dreaming, but one may be permitted to

doubt that he is. It seems far more probable that he has for a moment, without realising it, emerged at the waking surface of consciousness.

(Ellis, 1911, p. 65)

Perhaps part of the reason for the lateness with which lucid dreaming has come to be recognised as a real phenomenon, and as one worthy of the attention of philosophers and psychologists, lies in the difficulty, which we apparently all experience to a greater or lesser degree, of imagining that other people's subjective experience may differ in significant and permanent ways from our own. In other words, it may be generally under-appreciated that there are considerable differences between individuals on the phenomenological as well as the behavioural level. This idea was well expressed by Galton towards the end of the last century, in his book *Inquiries into Human Faculty*:

> In future chapters I shall give accounts of persons who have unusual mental characteristics as regards imagery, visualised numerals, colours connected with sounds and special associations of ideas, being unconscious of their peculiarities. ... It will be seen in the end how greatly metaphysicians and psychologists may err, who assume their own mental operations, instincts, and axioms to be identical with those of the rest of mankind, instead of being special to themselves. The differences between men are profound, and we can only be saved from living in blind unconsciousness of our own mental peculiarities by the habit of informing ourselves as well as we can of those of others.

(Galton, 1883, p. 32)

COMMUNICATION BETWEEN THE LUCID DREAMER AND THE OUTSIDE WORLD

In *Lucid Dreams* Green (1968a) suggested that, if lucid dreamers were as rational as they believed they were, it might be possible to communicate with them while they were actually dreaming lucidly. Perhaps it would be possible for lucid dreamers to learn to exercise sufficient motor control to signal to an experimenter. She also predicted that lucid dreams would be found to be associated with the 'paradoxical' phase of sleep, characterised by low-voltage, fast waves in the electroencephalogram (EEG), muscular relaxation, and the rapid eye movements – REMs – which have given this phase the name 'REM sleep'. One of the reasons given for this proposal was the fact that lucid dreamers often reported lucidity arising out of a preceding non-lucid dream, and the latter sort of dream had already been associated with the REM phase of sleep.

At first sight these two suggestions in combination present us with a difficulty, however. This is that in REM sleep the sleeper has no apparent control of his body. It is the association of this state of physical paralysis with an EEG similar to that of an awake person which has led to this being designated as a 'paradoxical' stage of sleep. (Moreover, in the REM stage, despite the apparent activation of his brain, the sleeper is paradoxically more inaccessible to external stimuli and more difficult to arouse than at other stages of sleep.)

The same solution to this difficulty was arrived at independently by two researchers, Keith Hearne working at Liverpool University (Hearne, 1978), and Stephen LaBerge of Stanford University's sleep research laboratory (LaBerge et al., 1981). The signalling method that both reseachers evolved depends on the fact that the eye muscles, unlike all other muscles during the REM phase, are, as the name implies, liable to be extremely active. It was found that if the lucid dreamer 'looked' right or left within his dream, this caused actual movements of a corresponding kind in his physical eyes, which could be picked up and measured by electrodes attached near the eye muscles. This makes it possible for simple messages to be transmitted. The dreamer can indicate by eye movements when he has become lucid, or when he is beginning or ending a task which he has been asked to carry out in the dream, and he can signal 'yes' or 'no' to a question which corresponds to a prolonged signal from the experimenter.

When experiments of this kind began to develop, the position of the sceptics incidentally became much less tenable. If it was possible to communicate rationally with a dreaming person, even if only to this limited extent, it was difficult to deny that he or she was what we would normally call conscious.

Experiments using this method of signalling by means of eye movements from within the dream suggested that lucid dreams do indeed take place, as predicted, predominantly during REM sleep; that they last from one to six minutes; and that they occur mostly in the early morning, towards the end of the sleeping period, when REM sleep is relatively abundant.

As a lucid dreamer is able to recall in the lucid state instructions which have been given to him while he was awake, he is able to carry out predetermined tasks. By this means it was possible to carry out experiments on the extent to which the lucid dreamer's waking report about the events in his dream tallied with the signals which he made about them while they were happening. From these experiments it appeared that the sequence of dream events which he reported as having happened when he woke up had indeed happened in the sequence that he described. An extensive series of experiments of this sort was carried out at St Thomas's Hospital in London, using as the subject Alan Worsley, who incidentally had been Keith Hearne's subject in the first successful eye-signalling experiments at Liverpool. For example, Worsley was able to draw triangles on the walls in his dreams, following the movement of his hand visually as he did so, and it was ascertained that this produced movements of his physical eyes corresponding to those which would have occurred if he had been following triangular movements in the waking state (Schatzman *et al.*, 1988).

Another finding has been that the length of the various parts of a lucid dreamer's experience corresponded fairly well with his or her subjective impression of their duration. For example, LaBerge asked his subjects to signal with eye movements every ten seconds, and though they were not perfectly accurate they achieved about the same degree of accuracy as a waking subject would have done (LaBerge, 1985).

Because the eye muscles are not in fact paralysed in the REM dreaming state, it is relatively easy to use them to confirm that the movements of his 'dream' eyes which the lucid dreamer makes within his dream correspond at least to a considerable extent to movements of his real eyes. It is more difficult to examine similar possible correspondences in the case of other muscles in the body. Nevertheless, other correspondences have been established between a lucid dreamer's dreamed movements and movements of his physical body. One experiment which was attempted, with partial success, was to instruct Alan Worsley to operate a kind of morse code by taking steps forward in his dream with either his right or his left foot. Although this did not produce a corresponding actual movement in Worsley's real body, it did produce nerve impulses which were picked up and amplified by electrodes attached to the feet. It was possible to ascertain that the electrical signals measured in his legs corresponded to the number of strides he was making in his dream, although his real legs did not actually move.

It has also been reported that his breathing rate can be altered deliberately by the lucid dreamer. In the relevant experiment, the dreamer's actual rate of breathing changed in accordance with the rate at which he made his dream body breathe (LaBerge and Dement, 1982a).

We will give further consideration to the phenomenology of the state which has been opened up to experimentation by the developments we have just described in Chapter 2. In particular we will consider some of the ways in which lucid dreams differ from the non-lucid dreams in which they are embedded.

Chapter 2

Lucid and non-lucid dreams compared

Although until quite recently lucid dreams have received little attention as a phenomenon separate from ordinary dreaming, the possibility of a dreamer being aware of his situation is occasionally referred to, at least obliquely, from classical times onwards (see LaBerge, 1985, 1988a for various reviews). This is not surprising if, as we believe, lucid dreaming is a forum of human experience which most normal people are capable of having. What is surprising, however, is that when this possibility is referred to, it is often presented as part of a discussion of dreaming, without recognition of the differences between lucid and non-lucid dreams. Freud, the great pioneer of dream analysis, was aware of the possibility of lucidity in dreams, but he did not apparently recognise that they may represent a quite distinct phenomenon from the point of view of psychiatric interpretation:

> There are some people who are quite clearly aware during the night that they are asleep and dreaming and who thus seem to possess the faculty of consciously directing their dreams. If, for instance, a dreamer of this kind is dissatisfied with the turn taken by a dream, he can break it off without waking up and start it again in another direction – just as a popular dramatist may under pressure give his play a happier ending.
> (Freud, 1954, pp. 571–2)

As will become clear, lucid dreams differ in several important ways from ordinary dreams, and whatever may be thought of the principles which govern the construction of ordinary dreams, those which govern the content of lucid dreams certainly need to be considered as a separate case. For example, although Freud may have believed that ordinary dreams are determined by a drive towards wish-fulfilment, they frequently contain elements which are grotesque or disagreeable. A lucid dream, on the other hand, may have a pleasant and liberating emotional atmosphere which few, if any, ordinary dreams approach. For example, one of our subjects writes:

> While walking along a lovely tree-lined avenue I realised I was dreaming, and a sense of peace filled me. It was an autumn scene, and the ground was carpeted with crisp, brown and golden leaves. Eventually the avenue opened into a brilliant sunlit glade; a sparrow alighted in my hand and I observed closely its natural appearance and the subtle colouring of the feathers. Surveying the scene I felt a sense of wonder that it was possible to behold – purely in imagination – such vivid detail and beauty.
>
> (Subject E)

In fact, it seems to us that lucid dreams are, generally speaking, much easier than ordinary ones to regard as the fulfilment of a wish for an experience of a certain kind. In many cases it is easy to imagine that the experiences provided conform to what a person might consciously choose if asked what he would like to dream about that night. In other words, there does not usually seem to be a need to invoke the distinction between *manifest* and *latent* content which Freudian dream analysts use in their inter-pretations, nor to appeal to mechanisms such as *displacement, condensation* and *symbolisation* as they do in explicating the wishes supposedly underlying ordinary dreams.[1]

The differences between the content of lucid and ordinary dreams would seem to be an interesting field for further attention by psychiatrists and psychoanalysts. A review of quantitative comparisons between the manifest content of lucid and non-lucid dreams has been made by Gackenbach (1988), which uncovered fewer differences than might be expected. Perhaps some method needs to be devised to study the different symbolic functions of lucid versus non-lucid dreams. As yet, little work has been done on this topic. However, supposing some method of investigating this question could be devised, we would suggest that lucid dream sequences may be found to represent wish-fulfilment at a level of personality closer to normal waking consciousness than that of ordinary dreams.

Empson (1989) draws attention to two other respects in which lucid dreams differ from ordinary dreams. The first of these concerns the feeling of being in control. As he puts it: 'When dreaming [non-lucidly] we are the spectators of an unfolding drama, and only rarely does one have the impression of being in control.' The lucid dreamer, by contrast, once having achieved insight, is unlikely to feel he or she is merely the passive victim of events, as he may do in ordinary dreams, and particularly in nightmares. He may even undertake deliberate attempts within the dream to alter its course or content, and thus gain control over the experience to a greater or lesser extent. We will be discussing the varying degrees of success achieved by such experiments more fully in Chapter 9.

The second point of contrast between lucid and non-lucid dreams to which Empson draws attention concerns the dreamer's degree of reflectiveness. Allen Rechtschaffen (1978) has highlighted what he calls the 'singlemindedness' of ordinary dreams, drawing attention to the fact that in normal dreams we do not usually reflect on our own 'stream of consciousness'. In waking life this stream may be said to be split into two components, so that one is both experiencing something and reflecting on that experience while it is still going on. This splitting of conscious experience seldom seems to occur in a non-lucid dream. The lucid dreamer, by contrast, characteristically does reflect on his or her experience while it is happening; indeed such reflections are one of the most characteristic features of lucid dreams.

Another deficit of ordinary dreams to which Rechtschaffen draws attention, and one which may shed light on the relationship between dreaming and mental imagery in the waking state, is the fact that one apparently cannot 'imagine' things within a dream. He writes: 'I cannot remember a dream report which took the form, "Well, I was dreaming of such and such, but as I was dreaming this I was imagining a different scene which was completely unrelated"' (1978, p. 102). As Empson puts it, 'Paradoxically, while dreaming [non-lucidly] we are without imagination' (1989, p. 92). Lucid dreamers, on the other hand, have found it possible to experiment with 'imagining' things within the lucid dream, albeit with varying degrees of success. In one such case (quoted in full on pp. 95–6) the attempt had the effect of disrupting the actual dream imagery. We shall be discussing the relationship between the imagery of lucid dreams, non-lucid dreams and waking imagination more fully in Chapter 6.

A final distinction between lucid and non-lucid dreams concerns their differing degrees of memorability. As is well known, it is easy to forget ordinary dreams, and people who wish to recall them often find it necessary to make a written record as soon as possible on waking, before any other concerns have an opportunity to distract their minds. By contrast, it seems clear that lucid dreamers do not suffer from the tendency to a subsequent loss of memory to anything like the same degree as normal dreamers (cf. Green, 1968a, Chapter 11), although this observation is somewhat crude and could be refined by further experimental work. It has, for example, been established that if people wake from ordinary dreams and are expected to tele- phone for weather information before they record their dreams, their recollection is likely to be seriously impaired (Empson, 1989, pp. 54–5). It would be interesting to carry out a similar experiment with lucid dreamers to see whether imposing a similar procedure immediately on waking from a lucid dream impaired his or her recall of it in a comparable way.

There has been much discussion of why it is that impressions formed during ordinary dreams are not well remembered. Empson follows Rechtschaffen in suggesting that at least part of the difficulty is due to the unreflectiveness of ordinary dreams. He writes:

> Our conscious control of attention between the reflective, evaluative stream of thought and the thinking essential to the task in hand is vital to our normal processes of registering memories. . . . The massive forgetting of [ordinary] dreams can be explained in terms of the strait-jacket of a single thought-stream preventing the formation of any . . . intention [to remember].
> (Empson, 1989, p. 92)

Empson quotes a remark which Erasmus Darwin made in 1794: 'We never exercise our reason or recollection in dreams.'

If this lack of critical self-observation is in fact the reason for the liability of an ordinary dream to amnesia, this would certainly account for the fact that lucid dreams are so much less liable to it. In a lucid dream a person is aware and critical of his own experience rather as he may be in waking life, although there may be limitations to this apparent rationality, as we shall see in later chapters.

Chapter 3

The pre-lucid state

A type of dream which is not properly lucid, but which is closely related to a lucid dream, is that in which the dreamer suspects that he or she may be dreaming and thinks about this question, or undertakes various tests, to try to decide the true situation. Green (1968a) proposed the term 'pre-lucid dream' for this type of experience. Although it is possible to enter a lucid dream state directly on falling asleep, or spontaneously from a non-lucid dream sequence, lucidity is often preceded by a pre-lucid phase of this kind. A pre-lucid dream may resemble a lucid dream quite closely in its degree of perceptual realism and in the extent to which the dreamer appears able to exercise his or her normal intellectual abilities.

The following is an example of a pre-lucid dream reported by Dr Moers-Messmer, a German psychologist. The dream has many of the characteristics of a lucid dream, in that it is basically detailed and realistic, and the deviations from strict realism which it displays are of a kind which are found in many lucid dreams. Although the dreamer begins by being unaware of the status of his experience, these deviations arouse intellectual suspicions in him. He reflects on the situation for some time before it finally occurs to him that, in spite of his reluctance to accept this conclusion, he is in fact dreaming.

> By a small river I am walking along a narrow path. I do not know the country, the place is strange to me. A woman is coming towards me and a large object like a hat-box falls from her grasp into the water and floats. The woman climbs down the river bank, steps onto the water surface, makes a few steps and fetches the object. This astonishes me and I leave the path

so as to go down to the river and look at the water. I have forgotten whether there were ripples, the colour is green and rather dull, the top layers are transparent. I step on it and walk over to the other bank. At each step I sink in slightly: it seems like walking on sand. Looking around me, I suddenly find the whole river covered with people who are walking across from the banks. The first surprise soon passes, I come to accept the facts as they are. But when I see a bridge at some distance, my unwearying intellectual curiosity stirs again. I begin to ponder: 'It cannot be ice; it is too soft for that and besides the air is too warm. Perhaps it is a new invention. But if so, why should bridges be built?' Suddenly I have a flash of enlightenment: 'Could it not once again be a question of a dream?' At first I feel a disinclination to accept this idea, but slowly convince myself that no other possible explanation remains to me.

(Moers-Messmer, 1938, Case 18)

Not all pre-lucid dreams end, as this one does, in the subject's becoming aware of the situation and entering a lucid dream. Even after the most careful consideration of the situation in which he finds himself, the pre-lucid dreamer may none the less come to the conclusion that he is really awake. There is therefore some degree of overlap between experiences classed as false awakenings (see Chapter 5) and those called pre-lucid dreams.

Pre-lucid dreamers may be convinced at once that they are awake by the solidity and realism of their environment, or they may proceed to various 'tests', the results of which may or may not lead them to draw the correct conclusion. It is interesting to consider some of the tests which are used by dreamers to determine whether or not they are awake.

The classic test of pinching oneself seems decidedly unreliable, as a pre-lucid dream is quite capable of producing a dream sensation of a pinch that is convincing enough to fool the dreamer. (For an example of a case in which this occurred, see McCreery, 1973, p. 15.) Indeed this seems to be true in principle of practically any sensation; we shall see in Chapter 4 that the apparent realism of sensations in lucid (and pre-lucid) dreams is, on the whole, very high.

Among the most successful tests used by lucid dreamers are: attempting to fly, tests involving reading, attempting to switch on electric lights, and tests of memory in which the dreamer tries to retrace the previous events which have led up to his present situation. Any of these tests are likely to yield results which are different from what would be obtained in waking life, and, provided the dreamer recognises the discrepancy, he or she may be led to making the correct inference.

On the other hand, the dreamer may well fail to spot the 'error' in the dream, as the following example illustrates. This dreamer remembers to carry out a test of his state by spinning, as in the waking state he has correctly concluded that when a waking person spins around, the spinning of the environment stops when he does and does not carry on under its own momentum. But in this dream, although he carries out the test, he is persuaded that the continued spinning is what normally happens when a person is awake.

I am walking with friends through a beautiful clear autumn landscape. . . . I say, 'Those claims about the completely realistic perception of the environment are quite untenable! How can it be possible that one could have the experience in a dream, for example, of this cold clear morning and brilliantly coloured autumnal forest in all its details? How could one feel in a dream the cold air in one's lungs when one takes a deep breath. . . . And these tests of reality are all eyewash! The spinning test for example. If I turn quickly through 180 degrees on the spot (and I demonstrate this) then of course the surroundings afterwards continue to turn in the opposite direction.'

(Tholey and Utecht, 1987, p. 87)

The following dream also shows some ingenuity in convincing the same dreamer, Paul Tholey, that he is awake, in spite of his attempts to think analytically. Dr Tholey is a psychologist, so the idea that he might be wearing inverting spectacles (which are sometimes used in experiments on perception in the waking state) is perhaps less implausible in his case than it might be in the case of most dreamers.

It occurred to me that a house directly in front of me seemed to be upside down, upon which I was convinced that I must be dreaming. But then I noticed that I had spectacles on, and it immediately crossed my mind that they might be inverting spectacles. In order to test this, I took off the spectacles, whereupon I saw that the house ahead of me was now standing upright. This led me to suppose incorrectly that I was really in a waking state.

(Tholey and Utecht, 1987, p. 88)

Often, then, there seems to be a considerable psychological resistance which is opposed to the dreamer's arriving at a recognition of his position. A particularly interesting type of pre-lucid dream is that in which the resistance expresses itself, not merely by suggesting to the dreamer ways of accounting for his perceptions, but also by modifying the imagery of the dream as soon as the dreamer becomes critical of it, as in the following example reported by the physicist Ernst Mach:

> At a time when I was much occupied with problems about space I dreamed that I was walking in a wood. Suddenly I noticed that the displacement of the trees was insufficient in terms of perspective, and deduced from this that I was dreaming. Immediately the deficiencies in the displacements were made good. Then again, in another dream, I saw in my laboratory a glass beaker filled with water, in which a candle was steadily burning. 'Where does it get the oxygen? There is oxygen absorbed in the water. But where do the gases which result from combustion come away?' Now bubbles began to rise from the flame, and my mind was set at rest.
>
> (Ernst Mach, quoted in Tholey and Utecht, 1987, p. 91)

A person having a pre-lucid dream may simply come to the conclusion that he is dreaming as a result of some indefinable, but unmistakable, quality in the situation. On the other hand he may expend considerable effort of intellectual analysis in his attempt to come to the right conclusion, as in the following dream reported by Moers-Messmer.

> From the top of a fairly flat unknown mountain I look out over a wide plain towards the horizon. The thought occurs to me that I do not know at all what time of day it is. I examine the position of the sun. It is almost vertically overhead in the sky and its usual brightness. This surprises me, as it occurs to me that it is already autumn and a short time ago it was much lower in the sky. I think: 'The sun is now standing vertically at the equator, so here it must be at an angle of about 45 degrees. Therefore if my shadow is not equal to my own height, I must

be dreaming.' I look at it: it is about 30 cm long. It costs me a
fair effort to regard the whole almost dazzlingly bright
landscape with all its villages as an illusion.

(Moers-Messmer, 1938, Case 12)

People who have recurrent dreams sometimes try to impress
upon themselves that they should realise they are dreaming
when the familiar dream situation occurs. However, it will be
seen from the following example that there may again be
considerable psychological resistance to the realisation, even if
the dreamer successfully remembers that a situation of this kind
should suggest to him the idea that he is dreaming.

I find myself standing at night in my shirt on an unknown
street. It occurs to me that I have often observed this before and
that I have long made up my mind not to be taken in by it
again. But it is not so easy to convince myself. I feel a strong
resistance to the thought and I am convinced that this time,
exceptionally, it is not a dream. I was going somewhere in a
hurry and there was no more time left to get dressed. I try to
think what I could have been in such a hurry about, but can no
longer remember. My suspicion increases again. As I pass a
lamp post I look down at myself and see that I really have on a
white shirt. I do not notice whether I have any shoes. Now I
make my usual test of dreaming. I take a run, jump in the air
and float slowly down. I experience once more the well-known
astonishment.

(Moers-Messmer, 1938, Case 14)

Stephen LaBerge has found the most reliable method for passing
from a pre-lucid to a lucid state in his own case to be a reading
test: he looks for some writing in the dream, reads it once (if he
can), looks away, and then re-reads it, noting whether it reads the
same on the second occasion as the first. He reports that in all his
lucid dreams it has failed to do so, and comments: 'Dreams are
more readily distinguishable from waking perceptions on the
basis of their instability rather than their vividness' (LaBerge,
1985, p. 123). We will discuss the question of 'reading' in lucid
dreams in more detail in Chapters 9 and 10.

The following is an example of a dream in which the subject
becomes aware that he is dreaming by speculating on his
philosophical or religious beliefs. The dreamer in question, Paul

Tholey, is a convinced atheist. It may be remarked that a dreamer's general philosophical ideas seem to occur to him relatively readily in a lucid dream.

> I find myself in a forest during a frightful thunderstorm. Lightning strikes a tree which is standing just by me. A large branch falls from it. Then I remember that, as a child, I always used to pray when there was a thunderstorm. Should I pray now? No – because if there were a God, he would certainly not think it of any importance whether I prayed to him at just this moment. And besides, he would have to show me by a miracle that he exists at all. At this moment the fallen branch stands up vertically from the ground, and flies up into the sky until it vanishes in the clouds. Does this mean that God exists? No! So it must be that I am dreaming.
>
> (Tholey and Utecht, 1987, p. 51)

One other test of dreaming may be mentioned: that of passing physical objects through one another. One of our subjects has found it a useful test to try to pass such objects as the handles of forks through one another, and the following two dreams are examples in which he carried out this test.

> I go up to a black man who's walking behind me and tell him that this is a dream. He seems disbelieving so I ask to demonstrate this to him. We go over to a skip. I take out two objects (one metallic, the other plasticky?) and pass them through one another, saying something like, 'There you are! That couldn't happen in real life, could it?' He is now more with me.
>
> A little later, his mates join him. They are white, all or mostly male, and heavy, potential fighter-types, so I am a little afraid.
>
> I ask them if I should fly to show them that this is a dream and they say, 'Yeah, yeah,' with much encouragement, so I do so.
>
> I am nervous and dubious but I kick off from the ground as from the bottom of a swimming pool. I rapidly (more than is comfortable) fly up past the houses to about thirty feet above the street and look down on the people below. I then descend, again rapidly and land quite hard on my feet in front of the group.
>
> (Subject N. C.)

Some time later I've 'woken up' in a place in America. It is a sort of 'dreamers' convention' – gathering of vivid dreamers. At one point I'm sitting on a bed. Have two toothbrushes. Wonder if this is a dream. Easily pass them through one another and realise that it is.

(Subject N. C.)

Although some pre-lucid tests seem to 'work' quite well in the sense that they lead relatively often to lucidity, it has to be said that there is no test which is absolutely reliable. Even if a test works for a time, the dream mind may perversely defeat the dreamer in the end. Thus, for example, jumping in the air has been found to be a fairly reliable test by some dreamers, as in a dream this usually results in the subject's floating slowly to the ground in a way that would be quite uncharacteristic of waking life. But one dreamer for whom this had worked for some time found himself falling in a most abrupt way, which was close to normal expectations.

We should perhaps note that in waking life it usually never occurs to us to doubt that we are awake, and if we deliberately force ourselves to consider the hypothesis that we might be dreaming, it usually seems to us self-evident that it is false. We certainly do not usually feel the need to resort to 'tests' of the kind used by pre-lucid dreamers in order to settle the question. It is interesting that once the dreamer has become lucid, he or she likewise usually needs no further tests to maintain the conviction that what he or she is experiencing is a dream. The proposition 'this is a dream' acquires the same sort of self-evidence that the proposition 'I am awake' usually has in waking life. (We say 'usually' here, since there is a class of waking experience which occurs under extreme stress in which the subject may be afflicted with a feeling that he or she may be dreaming.)

In view of the unreliability of the sort of mechanical tests applied by pre-lucid dreamers which we have described above, combined with the fact that we do not feel the need for tests when we are awake, McCreery (1973) has made the following proposal. If one finds oneself seriously asking oneself the question whether one is dreaming or not, it is likely that one is. This might at first sight appear as yet another 'test'; but it is really a proposal that one should try to remember that all tests are redundant. It thus has a sort of logical priority over other criteria. Stephen LaBerge tells us that he has given his subjects this idea with some success. The following is an account of a pre-lucid dream in which one of our own subjects, a practised lucid dreamer, remembered this observation, and drew the right conclusion as a result.

After a long ordinary dream I was suddenly standing outside a block of flats in which some of my friends live. A crowd of angry people was shouting in the street. Some of them had managed to force their way up the staircase that leads to my friends' apartment. I ran inside to see if anything had happened to them. All kinds of strangers were messing about in their apartment.

I spotted my friend Henrik, one of the occupants of the house. He was looking really sick: he was very pale, obviously hadn't shaved for days, and was now smoking hash!

This came as a shock to me, and the thought suddenly hit me: this couldn't be real – it had to be a dream. But it all seemed so real, so I didn't know what to think.

Then I remembered having read somewhere that if a person even considered whether he was dreaming or not, he could be sure he was. So this made me draw the (right) conclusion: this experience wasn't taking place in the waking state. But still there was some emotional resistance against facing this fact.

(Subject O. D.)

Chapter 4

Perceptual qualities of lucid dreams

INTRODUCTORY REMARKS

The lucid dreams with which we are most familiar are those of subjects similar to those on whom *Lucid Dreams* was based; subjects, that is to say, who have become fairly habitual lucid dreamers and have taken the trouble to make written records of their dreams. It is quite possible that people who become interested in lucid dreams to this extent have some natural aptitude for having them; and it is also possible that if they did not find such dreams pleasant, exhilarating or at least intellectually intriguing, they would not be motivated enough to develop them to this extent. When we offer generalisations about the qualities of lucid dreams they are based on dreams from subjects of this kind. Research on lucid dreams is still in too exploratory a phase for it to be possible to support all attempts at generalisation by reference to numerical analyses, but subjective generalisations have considerable value at this stage in pointing the way for future research.

It is possible that the dreams of habitual lucid dreamers of the kind mentioned form a particular sub-class of all possible lucid dreams. Sometimes in the literature we come across reports of lucid dreams which seem to us distinctly different in 'flavour' from characteristic members of this sub-class of lucid dream. It is, in particular, possible that as varied methods are increasingly developed for the induction of lucid dreams in people who may not previously have had them, potentialities for different types of dream may be being opened up; and we think that one should be careful not to assume that the characteristics of lucid dreams will necessarily remain exactly the same across what might be quite a wide continuum of varying types.

We are, then, going to base our observations in Chapters 4 and 5 on the lucid dreams of spontaneous lucid dreamers. 'Spontaneous' here means that the dreamers have more or less independently found ways of developing their lucid dreaming; they did not learn to do it by some method of laboratory induction, or intensive training in a system originated by someone else.

REALISM AND UNREALISM IN LUCID DREAMS

The lucid dreams of such spontaneous and habitual lucid dreamers are characteristically described as brightly and realistically coloured. On a 'visual' level, they may seem to be true to life in almost every detail. Subjects may examine their surroundings with interest, observing the forms and textures of objects, and sometimes finding that they appear impeccably realistic. They may also proceed to test them by touching them, and usually report finding the sensations convincing. Smell and taste are less common, but may be reported as also highly realistic when they occur. Pain, on the other hand, is distinctly rare and tends to be unsatisfactorily reproduced, as we will discuss below.

Examples of different lucid dreams in which various subjects felt the warmth of the sun, tasted wine, ate a plum, sampled ice-cream, and smelled the scent coming from a woman's hair, for the most part in apparently realistic fashion, will be found in McCreery (1973, pp. 15–17, 89–90, 110–11).

Examples of lucid dreams in which seemingly realistic 'sounds', in the form of music and singing, played a prominent role will be found in Chapter 5, pp. 49–51.

Lucid dreamers also report various bodily sensations corresponding to the movements that their body is making in the dream, or, in one case, the sensations appropriate to the dream action of breathing in cold air.

Examining the perceptual texture of the environment seems to be a characteristic activity of habitual lucid dreamers. The following example will illustrate this activity.

My wife and I are returning from a shopping trip in the city centre. At first, distracted by looking at the pretty flower beds, we pay no attention to the path. Finally it occurs to us that we are lost. We attempt to find our way and go down various side streets – in vain. 'But that can't be! In a place where we have been living for decades! It must therefore be a dream!'

No sooner have I come to this realisation than both the surroundings and my wife disappear. I however am standing in a room quite near a boy of about 12 years old. He does not move and only looks at me.

For a long time I look at his head and think that as it is a dream face, it is possible that the dream might have made a mistake in the anatomy. I must check this! I examine in detail the shape of the head. I start with the eyes, look at the mouth and nose, then the ears. I regard the little hairs, the lashes, the wrinkles – nothing is missing!

No sooner have I concluded my examination, than my self-awareness starts to dwindle again, probably on account of the exertion which this required.

(Lischka, 1979, pp. 80–81)

In the following example from Moers-Messmer, the imitation of reality extends, remarkably, to the seeing of a negative after-image from looking at the sun.

I am in an open square, surrounded by unfamiliar houses, when I realise . . . that I am dreaming.

First I observe the houses and their perspective, all as normal. I turn my head from left to right and back again, and the buildings slowly glide past my field of vision. They are clearly lit by the sunlight, and the sky is a brilliant blue, so I look for the sun, which at first I cannot see. Suddenly I see it, high up in the sky. It looks its normal size, and dazzlingly bright, and looking at it is uncomfortable, though not painful. Its brightness is evidently not as great as in reality, and I immediately compare it, as I look, with that of a carbon arc light or a several hundred watt bulb. When I again look at my surroundings, I see a bright spot before my eyes, while the periphery of my field of vision remains normal.

(Moers-Messmer, 1938)

In the first of the two examples above the subject's examination of his environment, or at any rate the visual aspect of it, fails to reveal to him any defect of realism; however, this is not always the case. The following account from Moers-Messmer illustrates how perceptual realism, in this case in a pre-lucid rather than a lucid dream, may appear to be complete in one modality (the visual) but defective in another (the auditory).

I am lying in an unfamiliar way on my stomach, next to various people who are sitting around and talking. Various improbable events which have just occurred have caused me to wonder for some time whether I might be dreaming or not. However, I am too embarrassed to try jumping up in the air in the presence of the other people, so I decide to observe everything closely and with circumspection, so as not to regret later missing an opportunity.

A wide meadow stretches out in front of me, with wooded mountains in the distance. All this is naturalistically coloured and brightly lit. The sky is blue and blindingly bright. The top-most trees on the mountains are clearly outlined against the sky. Despite all my efforts I can find nothing which leads me to believe in the possibility of a deception. Then I attend to my auditory impressions. The conversation I am listening to has a naturalistic timbre and volume. I can understand every word clearly. Nevertheless I have the impression that the words are seeming to emanate not from without, but from within myself, like audible thoughts. At this point it occurs to me that I am almost weightless, and am scarcely touching the ground on which I am lying. Just as I am about to concentrate on the contents of the words, everything suddenly becomes dark around me and I wake up.

(Moers-Messmer, 1938, Case 5)

A potential line of investigation would be whether some modalities are more prone to distortion than others in lucid dreams. For example, it might be that the visual modality is less likely to display unrealisms than the auditory, and the auditory less likely in turn than, say, the olfactory. This question could be explored, both by the analysis and comparison of accounts from a sufficient number of habitual lucid dreamers of their more spontaneous lucid dreams and by setting a number of such subjects standard tasks to be performed in the lucid state, such as eating ice-cream or smelling a particular sort of flower.

A further question that could be explored is whether verbal material, such as the conversation reported by Moers-Messmer in the example above, is particularly prone to distortion and unrealism. It is possible that the unconscious 'effort' required to produce an intellectually convincing conversation tends to be too great for the lucid dreamer. A comparable lack of realism is sometimes reported in connection with attempts to read written material in a lucid dream. For example, when the attempt is made to focus on written material it may be found to be blurry and unstable, as in the following case.

> I am looking at the display in a shop window and for fun I take off my spectacles in order to see whether I can still distinguish the larger objects. At first everything is blurry, and then objects become continually clearer. This astonishes me and I look at the street. As everything there is also clearly recognisable, a terrible suspicion comes to me. I run off, jump up and float above the ground and now I know that I am dreaming.
>
> As soon as I am on the ground again I run up to the next shop and pull the door open. Two people are standing behind the counter. I call out, 'something to read quick!' Books and newspapers are lying on the counter. I grab one up, leaf through it and read. I want to learn a sentence off by heart and read it several times through. The first half of the sentence does make sense, it is talking about the use of memos in business. The second half of the sentence is complete nonsense, even though the individual words are comprehensible in themselves. I particularly look for some newly coined words but cannot find any. On repetition the sentence seems to become continually longer although the content remains similar, and I cannot retain it in my mind. It strikes me that I am fairly tired and a strange indifference disposes me to do nothing more. The light is continually weakening, and in its place arise all sorts of fantastic images. Then I awaken and hear 3 o'clock strike. It is three and a half hours since falling asleep.
>
> (Moers-Messmer, Case 11)

We will be suggesting in Chapter 15 that during a lucid dream there may be a relative depression of function in the left hemisphere of the brain and relative activation of the right. If true, this hypothesis might help to explain the difficulty which lucid dreamers seem to experience with verbal material. The particular difficulty with reading will also be considered in more detail in the context of limitations on the control of lucid dreams (Chapter 10).

Admittedly, a characteristic activity of lucid dreamers within their lucid dreams is to engage in sometimes humorous verbal interchanges with figures in the dream concerning such people's ontological status, making remarks like: 'You're only a figment of my imagination, you know!'. However, it is possible that further research might uncover limitations on the dialogues that usually take place in lucid dreams, such as their length and the complexity of the information embodied in them.

It may be worth noting, incidentally, that the particular departure from auditory realism reported in the example on p. 25 corresponds to one sometimes reported by schizophrenic subjects with respect to their auditory hallucinations experienced during waking life, namely that the voices they hear are sometimes not fully externalised but rather perceived as 'within their head' (cf. Bleuler, 1911, pp. 110–11).

Subjects with failing sight have sometimes found themselves with their sight apparently 'restored' in lucid or pre-lucid dreams, i.e. having fully realistic 'visual' experiences (see, for example, Delage, 1919, quoted in Green, 1968a, p. 25). Similar phenomena have been reported in connection with both out-of-the-body experiences (OBEs) and apparitional experiences. One of our subjects, who described herself as 'rather deaf', and who wore glasses, reported that during an out-of-the-body experience she could apparently see and hear a play in a theatre she was 'visiting' perfectly well despite the lack of any representation of her hearing-aid and glasses in the OBE state (cf. Green, 1968b, pp. 129–30). Another of our subjects reported seeing the apparition of an old lady in a long white night-dress in his home, and said that he heard the rustle of her dress despite the fact that he was 'totally deaf' (cf. Green and McCreery, 1975, p. 169). The occasional occurrence of such a feature in all three states – lucid dream, OBE and apparitional experience – is an indication of a relationship between the three. This relationship will be discussed more fully in chapters 6–8.

Lucid dreams may also imitate various real visual deficits such as the blurredness of vision following the removal of spectacles. In one instance reported by Moers-Messmer, the visual scene first became blurred on his taking off his spectacles in a lucid dream and then gradually re-acquired definition and distinctness. It would be interesting to know whether this phenomenon, or others like it, are liable to occur in other subjects. In other words, do the unconscious expectations and general 'set' of the lucid dreamer, which are presumably among the factors determining the dream content in a case such as this, only operate over a relatively short time-span, gradually losing their effectiveness?

Lucid dreams occasionally exhibit a lack of stability in their imagery. Lischka (1979) refers to the shifting outline of a range of mountains in one of his lucid dreams, and other lucid dreamers sometimes become aware that when they have looked away from something within the dream for some time, it is no longer exactly the same when they look at it again.

Hands seem to receive particular attention from lucid dreamers, perhaps simply because they are one of the objects most often to be found near the subject's face when he comes to examine his perceptual environment in a lucid dream. Possibly there is also some connection to the fact that examination of one's hands in dreams is given particular prominence by Carlos Castaneda, whose books appear to be read by many who take an interest in lucid dreaming. There are several reports that attempting to focus on one's hand in a lucid dream may reveal it as being wrongly proportioned and blurred in places. In the following example the image of the hand seems to have been defective at one stage but impressively realistic at another.

> After realising I was dreaming I found my hands. I stared at them for a short while, and they blurred/faded slightly, so I averted my vision to a hallway or room I was in, then looked at them again. I became fascinated with my conscious directive of seeing my hands. The very lines in my palms were quite distinct, and I found I could stare at them increasingly longer without losing the image.
>
> (Marcot, 1987)

The reproduction of pain and physical damage generally seems to be avoided in lucid dreams, although sensations reminiscent of real pain sensations can certainly be reported. Subject E gives the following description of a lucid dream in which she tried to injure herself.

> I realised I was dreaming, and recalled my intention (formed a few days previously) to investigate the possibility of inflicting pain on myself in a lucid dream, preferably by knife. Finding myself outside a kitchen (unfamiliar to me), I entered and

selected a knife – then hesitated. For, although knowing I could not harm myself, and accustomed to immunity from pain in lucid dreams – nevertheless, deliberately to court the *sensation* of pain in this way seemed quite another matter and, I imagined, might well induce considerable pain. Gingerly I tried the point of the knife against my arm, producing a disconcertingly real sensation. I therefore experienced great reluctance to carry out my intention, heightened emotionally by the memory of a distressing news item (concerning stabbing) of the day before. However, someone came up and offered to cut a mole off my arm with scissors. I agreed to this but declined to watch, and presently she declared that it was done. I had felt nothing, but when I examined my arm the flesh, it seemed to me, had not been cut through at all, the mole hidden rather than removed . . . .

On awaking, I reflected that it would be wiser not to pursue this line of enquiry further, wiser not to go against what seemed an inherent principle in lucid dreams, and that I risked losing an immunity from pain by persisting.

The most realistic reproduction of serious pain and physical damage which has come to our attention is contained in the experience of Oliver Fox which is reproduced in McCreery (1973, p. 17). In this experience he describes being wounded, bleeding and half-blinded, with sensations apparently appropriate to such an experience in real life. It should be noted that some of the features of this particular experience of Fox's suggest that it might be classified as an OBE rather than a lucid dream.

The faults in perceptual realism which occur from time to time in lucid dreams may or may not be recognised as such by the subject while dreaming. Moers-Messmer, in one of the examples quoted above, was clearly aware at the time that his auditory impressions were unusual; and similarly one of our subjects noticed in a lucid dream that the telephone was ringing abnormally softly.

In other instances deficiencies in lucid dream realism seem to pass unrecognised at the time, or to be 'disguised' by the dreaming brain in various ways. For example, the difficulty which lucid dreamers often experience in reproducing the effect of a light being switched on (a topic discussed in more detail in Chapter 10) may be disguised by a switch or bulb being absent or appearing to be defective.

A subject may sometimes be impressed by the realism of his lucid dream at the time, but, on awakening and making a critical examination of his memories of the dream, consider that he was mistaken in considering this degree of realism satisfactory and decide he cannot have been fully 'all there' mentally at the time.

Among our own subjects, Subject C in particular has considered the question of the perceptual quality of his environment during a number of lucid dreams extending over a period of years, and invariably decided on waking that it was not equivalent to that of waking perception. On several occasions he has thought, while asleep, that he was finally experiencing a lucid dream whose perceptual texture compared favourably with that of waking life, only to revise this estimate on waking up. The following description is of one such occasion:

> Dreamt I was going along endless corridors. Thought: 'This is a dream.' Dream continued rather autonomously for lucid dream, and I thought, I must remember to repeat the purest form of the statement (i.e. 'this is a dream', and not 'this is a lucid dream' or anything else). Eventually came out into the open air and saw the sea in the distance. I may have thought, how nice to see in a dream what I would like to see in reality. Anyway immediately the sea was right close up, as if we were on the edge of it. (Illustration of the autonomy of this dream.) Instead of being calm and flat as it had appeared in the distance it was being piled into enormous waves by the wind. Then I was considering the texture of the scene and thinking, this is as good as waking life; at last I have a lucid dream in which the perceptual texture is indisputably as good as waking life; if I query this on waking it can only be because I do not remember it properly. The sun was shining on the waves and they seemed to be glistening as in reality, for example.
>
> I am in fact unimpressed by the perceptual texture in retrospect. It may be I don't remember it with the immediacy it had then. But it seems to me now that it is more that I was in a very un-complete mental state at the time – the dream just met all the criteria of vividness *in the dream*.[1]

In fact, perceptual texture is one of the aspects of his lucid dreams which has most occupied Subject C's attention while he has been having them, and on more than one occasion he has been impressed *within the dream* by its apparently realistic perceptual quality, only to decide on waking that this was a delusion, and that the dream was simulating realism, so to speak, rather than actually achieving it.

The fact that Subject C considers himself to have been deluded in his lucid dreams more than once by their seeming realism at the time might raise the question whether other subjects, such as Subject B, who are convinced of the 'perceptual' quality of their lucid dreams, might not have been similarly deluded without ever subsequently realising this. All one can say at this stage is that other lucid dreamers, for example Subject B, have carefully considered the question when awake and concluded that they have not been.

In the longer term, with the development of methods of monitoring the ongoing brain activity of healthy subjects, it should eventually be possible to verify the phenomenological difference, if any, between the lucid dream experiences of Subject B and Subject C, or others like them, by electrophysiological and other means. One may predict that the brain activity of Subject B during a lucid dream would be found to resemble more or less closely that of waking perception, at least insofar as the visual areas of the brain are concerned, whereas the brain activity of Subject C would be expected to show greater differences from that accompanying his waking perceptions, and would resemble more closely whatever brain activity is found to be characteristic of voluntary, waking imagery.

LUCID DREAMS AND WAKING IMAGERY

There are two distinct questions which may be raised concerning the relationship between lucid dreams and waking imagery. The first concerns the phenomenological relationship, if any, between the two. That is to say, is the imagery of a lucid dream in general like or unlike that of voluntary, waking imagery with respect to such dimensions as clarity, vividness, and similarity to actual percepts? The second question is, supposing that the quality of quasi-perceptual experiences varies from one individual to another, does the degree of vividness and realism of a subject's imagery in a lucid dream bear any relationship to his imagery in waking life and non-lucid dreams?

With regard to the first of these questions: the majority of the examples in the present chapter are from subjects who are implicitly or explicitly comparing the perceptual quality of their lucid dreams with actual perception in waking life, not with waking imagery, and reporting the comparison as favourable. By implication, the imagery of lucid dreams would appear not to be like that of waking imagery for the majority of lucid dreamers. However, we must recognise that there are some subjects who, even after a number of lucid dreams, when any learning effect might have been expected to have taken place, nevertheless compare their lucid dreams unfavourably with waking perceptions and regard them as being comparable to ordinary dreams or waking imagery. One such is Subject C, who despite having several dozen lucid dreams over a period of years, still considers that none of them differed qualitatively with regard to their perceptual texture from his everyday waking imagery or his non-lucid dreams, neither of which he regards as particularly vivid or realistic.

The possibility asserts itself that there may be wide individual differences in the degree to which the perceptual texture of lucid dreams may differ from that of non-lucid dreams and waking imagery, even among habitual and practised lucid dreamers. It would be interesting to know the relative frequency of the different degrees of perceptual realism attained by lucid dreamers, and whether these differences are related to personality differences in the subjects concerned. For example, might obsessionality or fear of loss of control inhibit not the occurrence of lucid dreams as such but their content and degree of perceptual realism once they have occurred?

Granted that there do appear to be individual differences in the degree to which the imagery of lucid dreams approximates to the phenomenological quality of waking perception, the second of our questions arises, namely whether there is any correlation between the degree of perceptual realism attained by a subject's lucid dreams and the degree of vividness of his or her waking imagery or the imagery of his or her non-lucid dreams. No work appears to have been done on this question at a group level as yet. Such indications as we have on this question in individual cases suggest that there is no necessary connection between the two. That is to say, a subject may have relatively unremarkable waking imagery but still have quasi-perceptual lucid dreams. For example, Subject B writes:

In my lucid dreams when I examined the surroundings they seemed to be completely realistic and I examined the shapes, textures, etc. in detail. When I remembered this in waking life it seemed to me that my opinion about the realism had been correct, as I had the same sort of memories of visual impressions and the mental processes of evaluating them that I would have had after a waking experience. In my first dream the surrounding environment seemed rather vague but a small object to which I paid close attention seemed clear and realistic. I have never thought myself to be particularly good at conjuring up vivid mental images, my mental imagery is fairly vague and nothing like the experience of really looking at a scene or a picture. However, I am supposed to have some artistic ability and might have been fairly good at drawing if I had ever practised. My lucid dreams were certainly nothing like any mental imagery I have in the waking state, nor like my ordinary dreams. The latter, as I remember them, are more comparable with waking mental imagery, being vague and largely abstract, in the sense that I have an impression of emotional associations rather than clearly defined visual images, although I sometimes retain fairly clear visual memories of some passages in a dream so that I could draw the layout of the setting or something I had looked at in the dream, but without the clarity and detail that my lucid dreams appear to have.

Two psychologists who were habitual lucid dreamers, Moers-Messmer and Embury Brown, both independently made a distinction between 'perception' and imagination in lucid dreams. This strongly suggests that their lucid dreams were phenomenologically distinct from their everyday imagery. Brown makes a clear distinction between perceptual experience in a lucid dream and what he calls 'dream daydreaming', by which he seems to mean the dream counterpart of imagination in the waking state. For example, in one account he describes sitting in a taxi in a lucid dream and thinking about an earlier phase of the same dream, an imaginative activity which he found dispelled his current 'perceptions' of the taxi. This case is quoted in full on pp. 95–6. In another example (quoted on p. 107) he describes sitting at his desk in a lucid dream, but imagining himself standing outside on the roof of his veranda. On this occasion the 'image' does not take the place of the 'perception' of the desk, and he continues to find himself ostensibly sitting indoors. Similarly, Moers-Messmer refers to an activity he calls 'introspection' in lucid dreams, which he clearly regards as something qualitatively different from 'perceptual' experience while dreaming.

McCreery (1993) has proposed that a distinction should be made between voluntary, everyday imagery of the kind most of us use on a routine basis in many of our cognitive operations, and largely involuntary, autonomous forms, such as hypnagogic imagery. It appears that the mechanisms underlying the two forms may be largely independent of each other, at least in certain subjects. For example, we have in our files the case of a subject who claimed to have no visual imagery at all as measured by the Galton 'breakfast table' questionnaire (Galton, 1883), but who nevertheless reported instances of involuntary hypnagogic imagery. Asked to think of her breakfast table and describe its illumination, she wrote: 'I don't see it at all. I am unable to see a picture at all.' Yet in answer to another question she wrote: 'When I close my eyes in readiness for sleep after I've said my prayers, I sometimes see pictures, they seem to be right in front of my eyes.' It is interesting to note that this subject also reported the following ecsomatic experience, which appears to have been visually quite realistic:

> I had the experience when I was 14 years old. I had been having a snooze, in the afternoon, after my first week's work [as a housemaid]. When I woke up I was floating under the ceiling looking down at myself, and saying I must get back, then all in a minute I was able to get up from the bed, but it was as real to me, as writing this letter.

Some allowance should perhaps be made for the fact that the experience had happened about thirty years before the time of writing this account. However, she later emphasised the visual clarity of the experience, saying, 'I could see the room in great detail, even the specks of dust', and remarking that this was despite the fact that she is short-sighted. Asked about the colouring of the visual field, she said that 'colours looked vivid and bright'.

In many subjects, particularly practised ones, the pheno- menology of lucid dreams seems to resemble that of the involuntary kind of imagery, such as the hypnagogic and hypnopompic varieties, rather than that of voluntary, waking imagination. The one notable exception among our own subjects is Subject C, who claims that the imagery of his lucid dreams aligns itself, at least in retrospect, more with his everyday, consciously directed imagery.

The question of the relationship between the quasi-sensory experiences of dreams – both ordinary and lucid – and those of ordinary waking imagery is one that has been of interest to a number of philosophers. They sometimes argue that dreams are simply a form of imagination in which the subject has lost insight, and fails to make any distinction between the contents of his or her mind and genuine sensory information. Mary Warnock, for example, has written that in dreams, 'the images take over. It is not that in a dream we confuse images with reality. We simply do not at the time have any idea that there could be two sorts of items to confuse. . . . In a dream there seems no distinction between the thought that something might happen and its "happening"' (Warnock 1976, p. 165–6). Warnock's model of dreaming, while it may be valid for some types of mental activity during sleep, does not seem appropriate for lucid dreams. The lucid dreamer is apparently able to carry on most if not all of his mental activities in parallel with having his quasi-perceptual experience without this necessarily having any direct impact on the content of the experience.

The quasi-perceptual type of lucid dream reported by Subject B and others suggests an affinity with hallucinations rather than with waking imagery. Slade and Bentall (1988, p. 23) propose the following working definition of the term *hallucination*:

> Any percept-like experience which (a) occurs in the absence of an appropriate stimulus, (b) has the full force or impact of the corresponding actual (real) perception, and (c) is not amenable to direct and voluntary control by the experiencer.

Criterion (c) would have to be qualified to some extent with respect to lucid dreams, since in many cases the lucid dreamer is able to influence, albeit to a limited and not entirely predictable extent, the course and content of the dream by voluntary control, as we shall discuss in Chapters 10 and 11. However, this control is often indirect, rather than direct, as we shall see in these chapters.

Hallucinations are to be distinguished from *pseudo-hallucinations*, which are characterised by Sidgwick *et al.* (1894, p. 76) as follows:

Pseudo-hallucinations may be defined as having all the characteristics of hallucinations, except that of complete externalisation. They are unlike the ordinary images of fancy or memory, which we voluntarily call up, in being spontaneous, and in being more vivid and detailed, and more steady. Like hallucinations, they cannot be called up, nor their form altered, at will. On the other hand, they are unlike hallucinations proper, in not seeming to the percipient to be perceived through the senses. It is with the eye of the mind, not the bodily eye, that he seems to see them; with the mental, not the bodily, ear that he seems to hear them; and accordingly they do not even suggest the presence of a corresponding corporeal reality.

Hypnagogic imagery seems to be generally of the pseudo-hallucinatory kind, though there are fully externalised exceptions. Schacter (1976) cites an auditory example of this latter kind in which an experimental subject, thinking that his name had been called, 'unhooked himself from the biofeedback equipment and ran into the hallway, only to realize that he had experienced an auditory hypnagogic image.'[2]

It is worth noting that the distinction between pseudo-hallucinations and hallucinations does not correspond to the distinction between experiences with and without insight, as has sometimes been supposed. Normal subjects may experience quasi-perceptual hallucinations with full insight (Green and McCreery, 1975). Like a lucid dreamer, the subject of a hallucination may consider the perceptual quality of his or her hallucination at the time of experiencing it and be impressed by its realism. We shall be discussing the question of insight further in Chapter 6, when we come to consider in detail the relationship between lucid dreams and other types of hallucinatory experience.

We think that overall the 'perceptual' phenomena of lucid dreams suggest a relatively high level of functioning of the right hemisphere of the brain during the lucid state. The finding that the right hemisphere is preferentially implicated in visuo-spatial tasks seems to be a relatively robust one. There is convergent evidence for this conclusion from very different methodologies. In the field of EEG studies, for example, Robbins and McAdam (1974) reported that the right hemisphere showed more activity when subjects were asked to generate visual images of scenes shown, and the left more involvement when they were asked to compose a letter about the same scenes. Similarly, in a blood flow study using a radioactive isotope, Risberg *et al.* (1975) reported relatively greater flow in the left hemisphere during a verbal analogies task and in the right hemisphere during a picture completion task. It seems to us that lucid dreaming is *par excellence* a visuo-spatial task. The subject is usually preoccupied with the visual field, whatever other modalities appear to be involved, and he or she is often moving around within that three-dimensional visual environment or 'space'. In the latter respect one might contrast the lucid dreamer with the subject of hypnagogic imagery, who is characteristically viewing the images as if they were a picture of which he or she is not a part.

Moreover, we think there are indications that during lucid dreams the right hemisphere tends to be more active or functional than the left. As we shall see in Chapter 5, although the intellectual operations and reflections carried out by lucid dreamers are remarkable compared with those that the same subjects would normally carry during their non-lucid dreams, they are not remarkable compared with those they could carry out in the waking state. By contrast, some lucid dreamers, such as Subject B, find it very hard to fault their imagery in lucid dreams when compared with their perceptions in waking life, and consider it to be of distinctly superior quality to the imagery they employ in the waking state.

Chapter 5

Memory, intellect and emotions

CONSCIOUS RECALL DURING LUCID DREAMS

There are certain methodological difficulties in arriving at ways of measuring the claims of lucid dreamers that they have a fairly normal degree of recall of their past lives and waking intentions while in the dream. Certainly there is evidence that lucid dreamers are able to recall intentions which they formed in waking life, or tests which they were instructed to carry out by an experimenter. But it is difficult to find definite methods for assessing the completeness and accuracy of their recall of their past life and present circumstances.

The only reliable way of assessing a lucid dreamer's ability to recall his past life would be to ask him questions while he is in a lucid dream state and to compare his rate of correct response with his performance in the waking state. Occasionally lucid dreamers spontaneously mention, after waking, some information about their past lives which occurred to them (apparently correctly) in a lucid dream. For example, Oliver Fox was reminded in one of his lucid dreams of his rank in the army by finding himself wearing the appropriate uniform. But these occasional spontaneous memories are clearly inadequate as a way of assessing the completeness of a dreamer's potential recall of the details of his past life.

We should like to be able to ask lucid dreamers questions while they are still asleep in a way that would test the accuracy of their recall of past events, but as yet no method of signalling to a lucid dreamer has been developed which would make this practicable. We have given an indication in Chapter 1 of some of the experiments that have been carried out on signalling by lucid dreamers from within the lucid dream; considerable progress has been made in this area, but the amount of information that has so far been successfully conveyed is small in relation to the present requirement. Signalling in Morse code to a lucid dreamer and receiving replies in Morse code as he looks to the left and the right in his dream is theoretically possible, but would certainly be cumbrous and time-consuming, so that only one or two questions could be asked and answered within a single lucid dream.

To accelerate the process lucid dreamers might be trained to recognise coded patterns of electrical impulses as representing specific questions. Thus, for example, a pattern such as 'short, long, long, short' might be supposed to represent 'What was the name of your first school?'. However, this method contains the difficulty that the subject, while memorising in waking life the pattern which represents the question, will not normally be unaware of the response. It is not usually possible for a person to rehearse a pattern of impulses which represents a question about their past life without simultaneously being reminded of the correct answer. In practice a subject who is learning a coded representation for a question will at the same time be rehearsing the correct answer, thus making the exercise of consciously remembering the answer in his dream somewhat meaningless.

INTELLECTUAL FUNCTIONING IN GENERAL

Some light may be shed on the question of memory in a lucid dream by considering subjects' intellectual functioning generally while in this state. In both lucid and pre-lucid dreams, people may find that they appear to be functioning fairly normally and engaging in quite complicated trains of thought, particularly in pre-lucid dreams when they are trying to determine whether or not they are dreaming. In pre-lucid dreams subjects sometimes draw erroneous conclusions, and this usually seems to be the result of faulty recollections concerning the current state of affairs in waking life. A person whose awareness of the circumstances of waking life was completely unimpaired would not spend time wondering why, say, a bridge had been built over a river, the water of which was firm enough to walk on, nor whether the unusually firm water flowing in this river might be a new discovery (cf. the Moers-Messmer example on pp. 14–15). In false awakenings, too, as we shall see in Chapter 7, dreamers may show an imperfect grasp of the conditions which are normally associated with the process of waking up. On occasion some irrelevant change in their circumstances, such as finding a pencil in their hand, may lead them to conclude that they are really awake now, whereas before they were not.

An intellectual limitation that seems to be displayed by a number of lucid dreams concerns the dreamer's belief in the relationship between the dream world, or elements in it, and the world of waking life. In some contexts a lucid dreamer may clearly display his realisation of the illusory nature of his perceptions, as for instance when he informs people in his dream that they are only figments of his imagination. However, we have encountered a number of cases in which the subject seems unwilling or unable to fully recognise that the hallucinatory world before him need bear no relationship to the waking world 'outside' his dream. For example, in a lucid dream of Embury Brown's quoted in Chapter 10 (p. 107) he speculates, while sitting in a chair by his desk, as to whether he might be sleeping in this chair in reality, and is surprised on waking to find that he is not. Of course, it is possible that Brown was in the habit of falling asleep at his desk, in which case his idea in the dream would not have been such an implausible one. However, it is more likely that this dream reflects a difficulty that subjects sometimes have within a lucid dream in fully accepting its total independence of the waking world. Another illustration of this is provided by a lucid dream of Subject C, in which he saw a telephone in his dream and wondered if there was a real telephone 'underneath' it in the real world.

It is possible that this intellectual limitation, when present, results from the fact that we are very habituated in waking life to implicitly assuming the physical world is really there when and as we perceive it. This may have the result that even when we are fully aware we are dreaming, it is hard to shake off the unconscious assumption that external reality is at least partially determining the form of our 'perceptions'.

It is interesting to compare this apparent inability of the subject in certain lucid dreams to shake off the assumption of external reality standing in some sort of relationship to his or her perceptual world, albeit in an unusual or indirect fashion, with the attitudes of apparition subjects to their experiences.[1]

West (1948) suggests that it is one of the differences between the hallucinatory experiences of schizophrenic people and those of normal people that the latter tend to have an insight into the nature of their hallucinatory experiences which schizophrenic people do not show. Having quoted an example of an isolated hallucinatory experience occurring to a normal subject, West remarks that it was 'recognised afterwards by the percipient as a subjective experience', and contrasts this with the fact that the psychotic patient 'often lacks the insight to realise the subjective nature of the experience, attributing it instead to some delusory external cause, such as waves of wireless or telepathy acting from a distance'.

However, in normal subjects insight may be said to show various gradations, or to be present in different degrees in different subjects. Complete insight might be said to be exhibited by Professor H. H. Price in the example quoted on p. 63 of a hallucination occurring under mescaline. Here the subject is aware that some leaves he is apparently seeing on his bedspread do not have the status of real leaves, and ascribes the whole experience to the abnormal functioning of his own brain due to the action of the drug.

Superficially, the subjects of apparitional experiences often appear to show insight of a comparable kind. As we shall see in more detail in Chapter 6, well over half of a population of 850 volunteer subjects who reported apparitional experiences to us said that they achieved insight, in the sense of realising that what they were experiencing was an apparition and not a real person or thing, before the experience ended (Green and McCreery, 1975). However, it cannot be said that the majority of normal subjects reporting apparitional experiences 'realise the subjective nature of the experience', in West's (1948) phrase, in the same sense that Professor Price realised the subjective nature of his mescaline experience. The majority of subjects reporting apparitional experiences, while recognising sooner or later that the figure or object they perceive (or have just perceived) does not have the status of a real person, nevertheless believe that it has some ontological status distinct from, say, the figures they see in their dreams. As Richardson (1969, p. 113) puts it: 'The percept-like experience is recognised as non-material, but is not recognised as being a subjective phenomenon.' Thus subjects who report seeing hallucinatory representations of deceased relatives usually imply quite clearly in their accounts that they believe the deceased person was really there in some sense, or at least responsible for their having the experience. To this extent, therefore, the normal subject hallucinating a dead relative ascribes his experience to an external cause in a way that may not be very different from that in which the psychotic subject does so.

It is also interesting to note that normal subjects who are experiencing a hallucination may express surprise that other bystanders did not share their experience. Bleuler (1911, p. 112) notes that 'Many schizophrenics not only believe that everyone around them can hear the "voices" as well as they do, but they also believe that even people far away can perceive them.' Clearly there is usually a distinction to be made between schizophrenics and normal subjects with regard to the corrigibility of the subject's beliefs about his or her experience. The normal subject is willing to be convinced that another person or persons who were in a position to perceive what he or she perceived did not actually do so, though he may remain surprised by this fact. It may not always be possible to convince a schizophrenic of this same fact. Nevertheless, the normal person may ascribe the unshared nature of his experience to his having some 'psychic gift' which those around him do not possess, especially if his experiences are at all frequent. In this respect he may not differ greatly from a patient described by Bleuler (1911, p. 112), for example:

> An intelligent hebephrenic, while we were talking to him, suddenly saw the devil standing behind him; and it was so clear and vivid that he could draw it for us. He declared, in response to our objections, that he just had the gift of seeing through the back of his head what was behind him. When he overheard us speak of 'imaginings', he protested vehemently that these were no imaginings but an actual ability to see these things.

The situation with regard to insight is also ambiguous in relation to out-of-the-body experiences in normal people. Most subjects are aware from the start that something anomalous is happening to them; for example, because of the unusual 'viewpoint' from which they seem to be 'seeing' the world, or because of the fact that they seem to be seeing their own bodies from outside. However, at least in our collection, which originates mostly from volunteers, the subjects often describe what they 'saw' as if they believe or assume it is true vision but from a new perspective. We

suggest that this is because what they 'see' is often phenomenologically indistinguishable from what they would see if they were
really where they seem to be (up near the ceiling, for example).

It seems that in both normal and psychotic people the constant
association of perception in everyday life with an apparently
independently existing external reality has the result that when
one experiences something that is phenomenologically indistinguishable from a true percept, there is a tendency, having the
force almost of compulsion, to think that there must be something
'behind' it in the way of a reality independent of one's own mind.

Normal, waking subjects may even show something less than
complete insight in this sense in relation to what have been called
pseudo-hallucinations. It may be taken as a defining characteristic of pseudo-hallucinations, such as hypnagogic images, that
the subject recognises that they are not 'out there' in the physical
world but 'in his head' or 'in his mind's eye', and to that extent
there is always insight into the subjective nature of the
experience. However, even normal subjects may attribute a
pseudo-hallucination to some external cause, in the same sense as
that in which they may attribute a fully externalised hallucinatory experience to an external cause. For example, normal
subjects may believe in a supernaturalistic explanation of the
origin of hypnagogic images. Sir John Herschel (quoted by
Leaning, 1925, p. 391) seems to have been tempted by such an
interpretation of hypnagogic phenomena on the basis of his own
experience; he suggested that they provide evidence of 'a
thought, an intelligence, working within our own organisation
distinct from that of our own personality'. Such a belief may
again be compared with the subject's belief, or implicit
assumption, in certain lucid dreams that there must be some
relation between what he or she is perceiving and external reality.

Returning to the subject of lucid dreams, in spite of some
deficiencies in certain areas, the state of mind and mental abilities
of a lucid dreamer clearly present us with something a good deal
removed from those of an ordinary dreamer. Ordinary dreams
are frequently confused, and narrative sequences which seem
reasonably coherent at the time can contain many incongruous
and disjointed elements which are held together only by the
dreamer's subjective impression that this is in some way part of
the same story. In fact, the linkage in non-lucid dreams may in
reality often be one which depends only on a fairly constant

emotional flavour. In an ordinary dream a person's memory of his waking life is very partial, although in a sense he clearly possesses some, since elements of his past waking experience, such as friends, relatives, or familiar places, may enter into the dream, and be recognised by the dreamer.

A striking example of someone attempting to test their own powers of conscious recall in a lucid dream is provided by the following example. While awake, the subject deliberately memorised the value of *pi* to sixteen decimal places, and then attempted to recall this figure in a lucid dream, with results he describes as follows:

> Dreamed I was walking and found my right hand. More often now, the dream-conscious state precedes my lifting my hand to my eyes, as it did in this dream. I recalled my experiment objective of reciting pi in a dream to test the extent of conscious recall, and did so. I recited it mentally; I did not speak in the dream, but consciously thought the numbers. However, as I reached the seventh decimal place, and was forced to exert greater effort to recall the numbers, I failed and rounded the number off at the seventh place, and stopped there. An instant later, in the dream, I was aware of what I did, but before having time to try again, I awoke.
>
> (Marcot, 1987)

It is interesting to note that the number of digits that this subject was apparently able to recall was roughly equal to a typical span that may be held by an average waking subject in short-term or immediate memory (Miller, 1956). Obviously one cannot draw any definite inference from a single case such as this, since the similarity might be purely coincidental. It might be that the subject was relatively familiar with the first seven digits of *pi* before he attempted to memorise the next nine. Further, the task, if carried out in the waking state, would clearly be one that involved long-term as well as short-term memory, and we have seen that there is considerable evidence that the subject can access a wide range of long-term memories in a lucid dream. So if there is any significance in the precise limitation displayed by this dream, it might signify some sort of failure of co-ordination between short-term and long-term memory. For example, having accessed as many digits from long-term memory as he could easily store in the short term, the subject may have been unable to access any more without forgetting the first seven.

Another possibility is that the limitation on this subject's ability in this particular dream represented a general difficulty with the recall of sequences of digits in lucid dreams. As already mentioned, we shall be proposing the hypothesis that the left hemisphere is relatively inactive or dysfunctional during lucid dreaming, and if this is the case the sort of sequential processing of numbers required by this subject's task may be relatively difficult in the lucid dreaming state, since the left hemisphere is thought to be relatively specialised for sequential as opposed to spatial or 'holistic' processing. At the very least, this case suggests a type of experiment that other habitual lucid dreamers might attempt to replicate, to see whether there appears to be any general limitation on the mental manipulation of numbers when lucid.

A methodological objection which might be raised to this test is that there is no objective verification of whether the subject recalled the digits correctly or not; we have only his impression on waking, which might in principle be erroneous, although this seems on the face of it less likely than that he should make such a mistake *within the dream*. One way round this difficulty would be to devise a test that would enable the subject to signal the nature of the digits in question while still asleep, though the length of time which such a test would take would encounter the practical obstacles we have discussed above.

The following is an example in which Subject C attempted to divide 200 by 5 in a lucid dream. At first sight his performance was less impressive than that of the previous subject, though here again it is quite striking that the dreamer was apparently able to think of a rational strategy for breaking up the computational task into manageable component parts, rather as he might have done in waking life. In this case the task was not one which he had set himself beforehand in the waking state, but was apparently thought of on the spur of the moment within the dream.

Said to myself 'This is a dream' repeatedly. I was standing on the point of a tumulus or hill in an autumnal landscape. I looked round. Looking in the direction of a country house I considered the problem of whether the picturesque scene really approached waking life in realism as it was pretending to do. I thought it did, and attributed my past scepticism in waking life to the effect of memory – it only seemed less realistic in retrospect because it was then a memory image one was inspecting, not the scene itself. (In retrospect it again seems to me I was wrong and that I was being gulled by something that was really only a dream of realism, as it were.)

Then, having left the mound, I tried to work out how many times 5 went into 200 to test my powers of calculation in the dream. I think I correctly remembered that 5 times 4 made 20 and then I planned to multiply 5 or 4 (I think I wasn't sure which) by the number of 20s in 200, but I think I wasn't really able to complete the operation to my satisfaction.

To summarise, the lucid dreamer tends to be intellectually 'present' to an extent which is remarkable when compared with ordinary dreams, but is liable to show certain deficits in comparison with his or her cognitive abilities in waking life. In particular there is occasionally evidence of a failure fully to appreciate the wholly unreal and inconsequential status of the dream content. We would repeat the conclusion suggested at the end of the previous chapter, namely that, taken with the remarkable visuo–spatial functioning of the habitual lucid dreamer, the data suggest a tendency to relative activation of the right hemisphere during lucid dreaming and a relative depression of activity in the left. We shall return to this topic in Chapter 15.

THE EMOTIONAL QUALITY OF LUCID DREAMS

The main point we shall be making in this section is that the emotional quality of lucid dreams is strikingly different from that of ordinary dreams.

It is not perhaps generally realised that studies which have examined the content of ordinary dreams in a controlled way suggest that they are, on the whole, not predominantly or notably pleasant experiences. Freud (1954) put forward the theory that dreams were determined by wish-fulfilment, but this basic idea needs to be applied in fairly complicated ways to provide an explanation for the majority of dreams. One table of dream research findings (Empson, 1989) lists the frequency of dream topics in a total of 473 subjects, and finds that dreams of being attacked or pursued, or of falling, are frequent. Another worker (Hall, 1953) classifies about two out of every three ordinary dreams as unpleasant in their emotional content, being characterised by such feelings as fear, anger or disgust.

It seems fairly clear that lucid dreams are based on somewhat different psychological processes from ordinary dreams, since the dreams of a habitual lucid dreamer scarcely ever contain unpleasant emotions of any kind, and range from neutral, through fairly happy and mildly interested, to positive joy, appreciation of beauty and an exhilarating sense of adventure. We do not have data on which to base a comparison with the lucid dreams of less habitual subjects, but from the literature on the subject the generalisation seems to hold fairly true that lucid dreams of any category are relatively immune from unpleasant elements. Isolated reports of disagreeable features may be found, but the emotional accompaniment is seldom characterised as disagreeable, and, where it is, other features of the experience sometimes suggest that the dreamer may have drifted into a non-lucid state.

It seems that the dreamer's insight into his situation, and his awareness that no real harm can come to him, guarantees a considerable degree of immunity from feeling in any way threatened by the dream environment. The generally pleasant emotional tone of lucid dreams may therefore be seen as related to some extent to the characteristic which we have just discussed, namely the superior intellectual functioning associated with lucid as compared with non-lucid dreams. At the same time one may wonder whether this intellectual functionality in itself entirely suffices to account for the fact that finding oneself in this situation so often seems to generate feelings of liberation, and of excitement at the prospect of undertaking adventurous explorations of the possibilities which present themselves.

The most clearly identifiable possibility of unpleasant emotion associated with lucid dreams seems to be that the dreamer might find his situation claustrophobic. Some people report realising that they are dreaming and wishing to awaken themselves, which occasionally results in frustrating struggles to do so. Reports of this type of experience appear to come mainly, or perhaps exclusively, from subjects who are not deliberately trying to induce lucid dreams, and any experience which could be classified in this way seems to be rare among habitual or deliberate lucid dreamers. (Of course, this could be because those liable to find the experience claustrophobic are unlikely to wish to repeat it.)

One of our subjects gives the following account of experiences he had at the age of about 5. It is interesting to note that later, in adult life, he developed lucid dreams without any experience of claustrophobia, but usually with a sensation of slight elation on realising that he was dreaming.

> Occasionally, on dreaming I would realise that I was, and as I did not much like my dream life I would stand away from the action of the dream, thinking how I could awaken. Sometimes I struggled to open my eyes and my inability to force myself awake was claustrophobic. I am not sure whether I ever really succeeded in awakening myself, though I think I once achieved an illusory success in opening my eyes.

This account is somewhat reminiscent of what students of sleep disorder have termed 'sleep paralysis' – a state in which the subject is mentally more or less fully awake but physically unable to move. Hallucinations apparently superimposed on the subject's real environment (i.e. his or her bedroom) may sometimes be reported in connection with this state (Schneck, 1957). We shall be discussing cases of sleep paralysis and their relation to lucid dreaming in Chapter 8.

Claustrophobia apart, it is difficult to find examples of unpleasant emotions associated with lucidity. A person who has been trying to have lucid dreams for some time is characteristically elated when he or she first achieves the necessary realisation in a dream, and this element of pleasurable excitement often seems to remain a common experience at the start of a lucid dream even with people who have had a good many of them.

We would suggest that lucid dreams show a lower degree of emotional complexity and 'loading' than non-lucid ones, which usually have a rather confused sense of unanalysed and only partially identifiable emotional cross-currents. In this respect, lucid dream experiences can approach waking life much more closely. The lucid dreamer seems to be insulated from whatever unpleasant preoccupations he or she may currently have, to at least the extent he is in waking life and possibly more so, whereas in non-lucid dreams the dreamer appears to be particularly vulnerable to such preoccupations, perhaps through not having available to him or her such conscious stratagems as distraction of attention.

In addition to the generally positive emotional quality of lucid dreams and their tendency towards elation and exhilaration, some people experience a sense of convincing significance in connection with both lucid dreams and ecsomatic experiences, and may even describe them as 'more real than any previous experience'.

Some subjects have experienced lucid dreams which appeared to them to be highly significant and to influence their waking life. Some may even describe certain of their lucid dreams as 'mystical' or 'transcendent'. Stephen LaBerge, for example, who carries out research on lucid dreaming at Stanford University, quotes a dream of his own:

Late one summer morning, several years ago, I was lying quietly in bed, reviewing the dream I had just awakened from. A vivid image of a road appeared, and by focusing my attention on it, I was able to enter the scene. At this point, I was no longer able to feel my body, from which I concluded I was, in fact, asleep. I found myself driving in my sportscar down the dream road, perfectly aware that I was dreaming. I was delighted by the vibrantly beautiful scenery my lucid dream was presenting. After driving a short distance further, I was confronted by a very attractive, I may say a *dream* of a hitchhiker beside me on the road ahead. I need hardly say that I felt strongly inclined to stop and pick her up. But I said to myself, 'I've had *that* dream before. How about something new?' So I passed her by, resolving to seek 'The Highest' instead. As soon as I opened myself to guidance, my car took off into the air, flying rapidly upward, until it fell behind me like the first stage of a rocket. I continued to fly higher into the clouds, where I passed a cross on a steeple, a star of David, and other religious symbols. As I rose still higher, beyond the clouds, I entered a space that seemed a vast mystical realm: a vast emptiness that was yet full of love; an unbounded space that somehow felt like home. My mood had lifted to corresponding heights, and I began to sing with ecstatic inspiration. The quality of my voice was truly amazing – it spanned the entire range from deepest bass to highest soprano – and I felt as if I was embracing the entire cosmos in the resonance of my voice. As I improvised a melody that seemed more sublime than any I had heard before, the meaning of the song revealed itself and I sang the words, 'I praise Thee, O Lord!'

Upon awakening from this remarkable lucid dream, I reflected that it had been one of the most satisfying experiences of my life. It *felt* as if it were of profound significance. However, I was unable to say in exactly what way it was profound, nor was I able to evaluate its significance.

(LaBerge, 1985, pp. 270–1)

LaBerge suggests that after some experience of 'wish-fulfilling' dreams, lucid dreamers may weary of dreaming the same dreams, and equally of being the same self, night after night. LaBerge writes,

It is at this point that the need for self-transcendence may arise. Such lucid dreamers no longer know what they want, only that it is not what they used to want. So they give up deciding what to do, and resign from deliberate dream control. Having recognised the limitations of goals determined by the ego, the lucid dreamer has surrendered control to something beyond what he or she knows him or herself to be.

(LaBerge, 1985, p. 269)

The following is a lucid dream reported by Subject E which the experient evidently considered belonged in the 'mystical' or 'transcendent' category.

I have had mystical experiences of varying quality in both lucid and non-lucid dreams, but the one which affected me most deeply occurred when I was 18. As I recall, lucidity faintly pervaded the initial stage of the dream, was lost, then returned with brief but devastating clarity following the culmination. Music drifted upon my sense of hearing, and in response I began skipping and dancing along the road, past some railings. By degrees the music took on a mystical tone, and I grew increasingly absorbed. Eventually, I wandered off the road into an open space where multitudes of people were assembled. Then, somehow, sense of time and self were lost, and I became one with the multitudes – our arms all reaching aloft towards the radiance, the music and the pealing bells . . . rejoicing for evermore . . . but then intruded a grievous sense of being drawn away, of falling back to earth . . . and I couldn't bear to leave that bliss . . . but inexorably I was waking up.

As an atheist, I am not inclined to interpret this 'peak experience' in religious terms but rather as an intimation of the next level of being – i.e. beyond 'self' in the evolutionary hierarchy: matter, life, consciousness, self.

We shall be arguing in Chapters 7 and 8 that there is a close relationship between lucid dreams and out-of-the-body experiences. It is therefore interesting to note that exhilaration and elation are also occasionally found in out-of-the body experiences (see Green, 1968b). Some accounts of OBEs, indeed, also resemble accounts of 'mystical' experiences.

Not all lucid dreamers report dreams which they find so emotionally significant as the two quoted above, and it is possible that only certain types of personality are likely to have such experiences. Research on the content of lucid dreams and their relation to determining factors in the dreamer's personality is still at an early stage of development.

Fenwick (1984, 1987) has argued that the right temporal lobe of the brain is particularly involved in the mediation of mystical or ecstatic experience. This view is derived in part from the study of certain patients with epilepsy involving the right temporal area who report such experiences. If this view is correct, the occurrence of such experiences in the lucid dream state may be another indication that the right hemisphere of the brain is liable to be preferentially activated in such dreams.

Chapter 6

Lucid dreams and other hallucinatory experiences

INTRODUCTION

Lucid dreams occupy a key position in the range of hallucinatory experiences which we have been studying at the Institute of Psychophysical Research.

When the Institute was founded in 1961 there were tantalising hints of a wide range of paradoxical phenomena, including lucid dreams and out-of-the-body experiences, which appeared to have important implications for the study of normal perception. Our first attempts at clarification, however, took place in an atmosphere of great uncertainty. A few people had published accounts of their own lucid dreams, but no one had yet recognised this class of phenomena or attempted to define the characteristics which the lucid dreams of different people had in common. With regard to out-of-the-body experiences a number of cases had been reported, but these had been viewed mainly as providing support for spiritualistic theories and beliefs, or as providing possible evidence for the occurrence of extrasensory perception.

Lucid Dreams (Green, 1968a) was written at a time when there was little or no recognition of the potentialities which this topic might have for opening up a developing field of research, and our public appeals for cases of out-of-the-body and hallucinatory experiences were undertaken in an exploratory spirit, with little certainty that the public would respond to appeals of this nature in any significant numbers.

However, as it happened, it emerged that our work in all these fields was making contact with a stratum of human experience which is now increasingly recognised as likely to form a stable

and consistent part of psychological and physiological functioning, and which, by its paradoxical nature, may well lead to
fundamental insights into the processes of sleeping and waking,
and the relationship of the conscious mind to the environment as
it perceives it.

As we noted in Chapter 1, it is a fairly remarkable fact that
lucid dreams have received so little attention through the
centuries as a type of experience which has quite different characteristics from ordinary dreaming. It is the more remarkable
because most lucid dreamers find the experience a pleasurable
and interesting one, and it is relatively easy for people who wish
to have lucid dreams to develop them. In fact, as we will see in
Chapter 11, one of the most remarkable features of lucid dreams
is their responsiveness to deliberate development. The mere fact
of being aware of the possibility of lucid dreams may be sufficient
for a person to start having them, while on the other hand few
people become habitual or frequent lucid dreamers without some
degree of deliberate effort or intention.

Nevertheless, it is possible that some kinds of subjects have a
particular aptitude in this direction. People who are prone to
lucid dreams often report ecsomatic experiences and related
phenomena as well as lucid dreams. This may have been one of
the reasons why lucid dreams remained for so long unrecognised
as a distinct category of dream experience. Books which included
accounts of lucid dreams, such as Oliver Fox's *Astral Projection*
(1962) or J. H. M. Whiteman's *The Mystical Life* (1961), often
included accounts of out-of-the-body experiences as well. This
may have meant that lucid dreams were rejected by association
with the theories of spiritualism, and in particular the theory that
an out-of-the-body experience is to be regarded as a 'projection'
of an 'astral body', or the transport of the subject's soul into a
purely spiritual dimension.

The study of lucid dreams made us aware of some other types
of anomalous experience. One of these is the pre-lucid dream,
discussed in Chapter 3, which seems to differ from a lucid dream
principally in the lack of full realisation of the dreamer's position.
In this type of dream, as we have seen, the dreamer asks himself
whether or not he may be dreaming, and he may or may not come
to the correct conclusion (that he is).

Another form of anomalous experience which occurs in
association with lucid dreams is the false awakening. This may

occur following both lucid and non-lucid dreams, and in its
commonest form consists in the subject seeming to wake up, only
to discover subsequently that this 'waking' process was still part
of a dream. This discovery may occur while he or she is still
asleep, in which case a lucid dream may ensue, or it may not
occur until the subject really wakes up. The following extract
from an account of a lucid dream will provide an example of the
latter sort.

> Eventually someone loomed up above me (I was still on my
> hands and my knees, as it were, looking at the floor) and asked
> me, 'What is your name?' I thought: 'That will wake me up',[1]
> but nevertheless for some reason I decided to answer and
> called out my name, throwing back my head and laughing, as
> if the decision not to worry any more about mantaining the
> lucidity and to wake up was somewhat reckless or abandoned.
> With that thought I woke up, and I thought: 'I must go and
> make notes of the lucid dream.' However, I seemed rather
> vague as to where I should go to do this (I was still in the same
> place, in the hall) and there followed a short non-lucid dream
> from which I woke properly a short time after.
> When I properly awoke I thought: 'Quelle surprise! I thought
> I had already woken up.'

The phenomenon of the false awakening will be discussed in
more detail in Chapter 7.

All the forms of totally hallucinatory experience which we
have mentioned may be regarded as closely related. Pre-lucid
dreams may turn into lucid ones, and some habitual subjects
have claimed that it is possible to pass from a false awakening to
a lucid dream, and from a lucid dream or some type of false
awakening to an out-of-the-body experience. Indeed, some
subjects have regarded certain types of false awakening as
equivalent to out-of-the-body experiences.

Figure 6.1 attempts to give a schematic summary of the relationships between these various sorts of totally hallucinatory
experience. Overlapping of ellipses indicates that the categories of
experience represented overlap to some extent, and arrows indicate
that the one type of experience may give rise to the other. It will be
seen that false awakenings (particularly the 'Type 2' false
awakening to be discussed in Chapter 7) seem to be particularly
versatile in their potential development. They may develop into

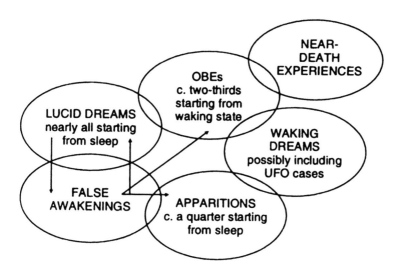

Figure 6.1 Relationships between various metachoric experiences (environment completely hallucinatory)

Source: Green, 1990

lucid dreams, out-of-the-body experiences, or a third form of hallucinatory phenomenon, namely apparitional experiences. We will now discuss the latter category in more detail.

THE CONCEPT OF METACHORIC EXPERIENCES

In 1968 we made an appeal for cases of apparitions; that is, cases in which a hallucinatory figure or object is apparently superimposed on the otherwise normal perception of the environment. When we began our study of these cases we were already acquainted with a considerable range of experiences, such as lucid dreams and ecsomatic experiences, which were capable of providing a convincing replica of normal life and which could be entered with little or no awareness that a discontinuity with normal experience had taken place. These experiences provided an extension of the previous idea of a hallucination as an isolated area of perceptual anomaly which was supposed to be superimposed upon, and in some way generated by a different process from, the world of normal perception.

As a result of our study of the apparitional cases we received, this range of totally hallucinatory experiences was extended still further. We already knew that in a false awakening a person might see 'apparitional' monsters or figures of various kinds, although in fact the whole of the visual field was hallucinatory. However, the study of the apparition cases which we received led us to the idea that many apparitional experiences, and perhaps all of them, were analogous to lucid dreams and OBEs in being totally hallucinatory. We proposed the adjective *metachoric* to designate experiences of this type, in which the normal perceptual environment is entirely replaced by a hallucinatory one, which may on occasion be a convincing replica of the world of normal perception (Green and McCreery, 1975).[2]

Apparitions may be characterised as hallucinations which are (a) 'projected' on to the external world and (b) consist of unrealistic or non-existent elements which appear more or less fully integrated into the rest of the perceptual field. On the face of it the latter component, the apparently veridical representation of a greater or lesser part of the subject's physical environment, consists of normal percepts based on sensory input. This seems to be the interpretation of the situation assumed by the philosopher C. D. Broad (1962), for example. He contrasts dreams and apparitional experiences in the following terms. He writes of dreams: 'The whole context is hallucinatory, though certain features in it may ultimately originate in specific sensory stimuli from within or without the dreamer's body' (p. 191). He contrasts with this the situation of the sane person in good health who suddenly has what he calls 'an hallucinatory *quasi*-perception' when he is wide awake. Here, writes Broad, 'the principal figure, and possibly some of its immediate appurtenances, are hallucinatory; but the background is usually that of normal waking sense-perception.'

It is perhaps not entirely clear from these remarks whether Broad is merely describing the empirical facts of the situation, namely that some of what the percipient is seeing corresponds to the physical environment and some of it does not, or whether he is asserting a qualitative or philosophical difference in status between the figure of the apparition and the background environment. However, this very ambiguity perhaps indicates that there is an area of unanalysed assumption in what one might call the conventional view of hallucinations, namely that it is only the unrealistic or non-existent element that is hallucinatory while the rest of the environment continues to be perceived normally.

The conventional view seems also to have been held, at least implicitly, by the authors of one of the earliest studies of hallucinations in the sane, that of Sidgwick *et al.* (1894, p. 75), who wrote of the person perceiving an apparition:

> [T]he percipient, while experiencing the hallucination, is at the same time normally perceiving real objects within his range of vision, and the hallucinatory percept is brought into relation with these, so as to occupy apparently as definite a place in the field of vision. The phantasm appears to stand side by side with real objects.

In contrast to these views, we have suggested (Green and McCreery, 1975) that the whole visual field may be hallucinatory in such experiences, and not just the unrealistic or non-existent element.

This interpretation is clearly indicated in a case such as the following, which is taken from our collection. It is of the 'waking dream' type, in which the subject's normal perceptual environment was temporarily completely displaced by a hallucinatory one. The subject was a New Zealander and the experience took place on a visit to England, when she went to stay at what had once been a priory.

> On arrival, a lady in charge took us through the entrance hall, and opened a door on the far side, right on [the] banks of [the] river. As we stood in the afternoon sunshine, suddenly everything was black and rain seemed to be slanting down, and there was a small boat, and seven or eight figures in flapping black clothes, hurrying to get into the building – there was a great feeling of *fear*. I was surprised to find shortly that I still stood in the afternoon sun.

We will not attempt to rehearse here all the considerations which led us to suggest that in a sense all apparitional cases may be of the waking dream type, with a complete substitution of the perceptual environment with a hallucinatory one. For a full account we would refer the interested reader to the first five chapters of our book *Apparitions* (Green and McCreery, 1975). However, we will mention one other class of apparitional case in which the metachoric interpretation is clearly indicated, and that is the class of those in which the illumination of the whole environment appears altered during the experience. The following is a case of this type:

> On New Year's Eve, 1852, I awoke about 12.40 a.m. and found my room so brilliantly illuminated that I imagined I had forgotten to put out my candle, and that something must have caught fire. I got up and, on looking round, saw at the foot of the bed a coffin resting on chairs, on each of which was a silver candlestick with a large wax taper alight; in the coffin was a figure of my father. I put out my hand and touched him, when it became quite dark. I felt for my matchbox and lighted a candle, looked at my watch and wrote down the time. The next morning I told a friend, with whom I was staying in Paris at the time, and on the morning of the 2nd of January we received a letter from Marseilles, saying that my father had died suddenly at 12.40 on New Year's Eve, and that he had expressed such a strong wish to see his youngest child (i.e., myself) again just before his death.
>
> (Gurney et al., 1886, Vol. I, pp. 436–7)

Clearly, in a case such as this, the whole scene is hallucinatory until the room 'becomes dark', even though the representation of the room may have been realistic except for certain elements such as the coffin and the candles. That is to say, apart from those added elements, the subject may have 'seen' the room much as it was at the time.

What we propose as a hypothesis is that many, if not all, apparitional experiences are of the metachoric type, like the two quoted above, even when a large part of the subject's visual environment appears to him or her to remain unchanged throughout the experience, and there is no obvious clue to give away the hallucinatory status of these unchanged parts, such as an apparent change in the overall level of illumination.

Employing the philosophical device of Occam's razor may be appropriate here. The situation is that there is a minority of cases of waking hallucination in which the metachoric hypothesis is forced upon us, as in the two cases just quoted. As far as we can see there are no cases in which the metachoric interpretation is impossible and the conventional interpretation the only possible one. Therefore, to retain the conventional interpretation in those cases where the metachoric one is not forced upon us requires us to postulate two distinct kinds of mechanism, the one metachoric and the other 'partial', for what appears to be a relatively homogeneous class of experience. For example, it would appear to be a relatively contingent matter that the hallucinatory lighting affects the whole scene in the second case, and not just part of it, as in the majority of hypnopompic apparitions. Similarly, it seems a relatively inessential feature of the first case that the whole visual environment is temporarily replaced with a hallucinatory one, rather than only part of it as in those cases in which only a figure is 'seen'. By contrast, to adopt the metachoric interpretation for all cases involves us in postulating only one basic hallucinatory process behind the whole class of experiences.

It does not seem to have been generally realised that what we have called the conventional view of hallucinations, as expressed or implied by Professor Broad and the Sidgwick report quoted above, poses a serious theoretical difficulty. This is the question of how the hallucinatory percept of an apparitional figure is integrated with the apparently normal percepts of the environment surrounding it.

If the hallucinated subject is continuing during his hallucination to perceive most of his environment in the normal way and hallucinating only a part of his visual field, for example, that occupied by a human figure which is not really there, then in many cases this would seem to involve us in positing the occurrence of two kinds of hallucination at once, a negative as well as a positive one. The reason for this is that many hallucinatory experiences in normal people involve opaque-seeming rather than transparent hallucinatory elements. For example, we found that 91 per cent of our subjects reporting apparitional experiences, when questioned on the degree of apparent transparency of what they had seen, described the apparition as looking completely opaque like a normal object so that nothing was visible through it, rather than transparent so that they could see what was behind it. In many cases, therefore, we have to explain why the hallucinatory element appears to 'block out' that part of the real environment which lies 'behind' it.

One way we could explain this is to suppose that the subject has a negative hallucination for the part of the environment behind the hallucinatory figure. Horowitz (1975) seems to be referring to this possibility when, defining hallucinations, he writes: 'The "ideal" hallucination, according to Esquirol's (1838) strict definition,[3] is independent of immediate external information except as external information is "negatively hallucinated" to allow conceptual "space" for (the externalized) information of internal origin.'

However, Horowitz does not seem to have appreciated the difficulties this model would raise. On this view of the matter we should also have to suppose in many cases that the negative hallucination moves and changes its configuration in such a way as continually to coincide with just that part of the visual field which is occupied by the positive hallucination. Sidgwick *et al.* (1894) noted that in more than half of their visual cases the hallucinatory figure was seen to move in various ways. Likewise we found that 66 per cent of our own subjects, when asked, reported that the apparition moved in some way in relation to the rest of the visual environment.

The failure to notice this problem may partly result from the relative neglect of hallucinatory experiences in the sane, and the corresponding focus on the hallucinations of the mentally ill. The latter appear to be predominantly auditory, at least in the forms which most often attract the attention of physicians, and in the auditory modality the problem of integration is less obvious. The fact that hallucinations in mental illness often occur in the context of other symptoms, such as delusional beliefs, may also have tended to distract attention away from the phenomenology of the experiences themselves, or at any rate made such a study difficult compared with the comparable enterprise in relation to the hallucinations of the sane.

The only writer we have come across who has clearly articulated the problem of how hallucinations and normal percepts are integrated is the pioneer electroencephalographer, W. Grey Walter. He illustrates the problem by reference to the case of an epileptic patient he studied.

Another patient, who was referred to our clinic in Bristol during the war with a shell wound in the posterior part of his left temporal lobe, had attacks preceded by a vision of an ugly old crone dressed in rags and . . . emitting a disagreeable smell, who would clatter about in the kitchen, apparently cooking some unsavoury dish. He was alarmed by this recurrent vision which resembled the witch of a fairy tale, but as she seemed to mean no harm he accepted her as a familiar, and mentioned that – apart from her ragged clothes and odour – she rather resembled his grandmother.

(Walter, 1960, pp. 5–6)

As Walter points out, in a case such as this the brain region affected is such as to involve disturbance of three sensory modalities at once – vision, hearing and olfaction – as well as the evocation of affective elements. He writes:

> The difficulty in such cases is to explain how the brain lesion could produce so integrated a pattern of illusion, in which the neurogenic components, the crocodile or the crone, were projected precisely on the physical background so as to take their place within the framework of external reality. Illusory figures of this sort will often come through a doorway, sit on a chair, use an implement and yet be appreciated sooner or later as illusory or unreal.

(Walter, 1960, pp. 6–7)

The necessity of positing two separate but simultaneous hallucinatory processes, the positive and the negative, to account for certain types of visual experience is removed if we adopt the metachoric interpretation. Experiences in which the hallucinatory element appears integrated into the subject's real environment do not present a special problem for such a view, regardless of whether the hallucinatory element appears opaque or transparent. If the whole scene is hallucinatory then there seems no *a priori* reason why the one unrealistic element, that is, the apparitional figure, should not appear opaque rather than transparent. That it is relatively 'easy' for a person to hallucinate the entire field of vision, and in such a way as to convince the subject that he is seeing his actual environment, is demonstrated by experiences such as false awakenings and out-of-the-body experiences.

If the present model of apparitional experiences is correct, then, there are at least four types of metachoric experience: lucid dreams, false awakenings, out-of-the-body experiences and apparitional experiences.

In general, we believe that the metachoric interpretation resolves the problem that Grey Walter raises of how purely hallucinatory perceptions are integrated with input-based perceptions. If we regard the whole field of vision as hallucinatory during, for example, the aura preceding the epileptic attacks of Grey Walter's patient, then the problem of integration does not arise.

The metachoric model of waking hallucinations suggests that they may have a closer relationship with lucid dreams than might otherwise appear. Thus in both types of experience the subject is surrounded by a completely hallucinatory environment, the difference being that in lucid dreams this is initiated during sleep whereas during an apparitional experience it is initiated from the waking state.

THE QUESTION OF INSIGHT

It might be suggested that a further difference between a lucid dream and an apparitional experience is that the lucid dreamer, by definition, has insight into the hallucinatory nature of his or her experience, whereas the subject of hallucinations starting from the waking state does not. However, our study of hallucinations reported by ostensibly normal people suggested that such subjects do not necessarily lack insight into the hallucinatory nature of their experience. We have already discussed this question to some extent in Chapter 5. Our data suggested that people's self-rating of the timing of insight in relation to the hallucinatory experiences was extremely variable. Table 6.1 gives the results of a questionnaire item on this point in our sample of 850 volunteer subjects. People were asked to choose one of four alternatives to describe the point at which they achieved insight into the apparitional nature of their experiences.

Table 6.1 Points of insight in apparitional experiences

Point of insight	Percentage of subjects
Immediately they started to perceive the apparition	46
Not immediately, but before they stopped perceiving it	18
As it ended	5
Not until after it ended	31

Source: Green and McCreery, 1975

It will be seen that nearly half the subjects realised immediately that what they were perceiving was not a real object or person.

An interesting example of apparently complete insight during a hallucination starting from the waking state was reported by the philosopher H. H. Price in connection with a mescaline experience.

> Strictly speaking, it was a partial hallucination, since it affected only a part of the visual field, and the rest of the visual field remained perfectly normal. It happened rather late in the day, in twilight. I was sitting on a chair looking at a divan bed. The bedspread covering it had a very well-marked pattern, with strong contrasts between the lighter and the darker parts. Quite suddenly the bedspread appeared to turn into a pile of very large dead leaves. They were curious leaves, like holly leaves in shape, but very much larger, perhaps three times as large. . . . The shapes of the leaves were very clear and vivid. The whole pile, and each leaf in it, was markedly three-dimensional, if anything more solid looking than a real pile of dead leaves would have been. Unlike the occasional minor visual hallucinations which most of us have probably experienced at one time or another, this was not brief and fugitive. It did not pass away so quickly that one hardly had time to notice it. On the contrary, this hallucination continued for quite a long time, two or three minutes perhaps, without any noticeable change. I had ample leisure to study it and enjoy it. Contrary to what some philosophers have suggested, my judgment was not in the least confused. I did not suppose for a moment that the leaves were really there, though they *looked* as real as could be. I was perfectly well aware all the time that the experience was hallucinatory and greatly delighted by it for just that reason.
>
> (Price, 1964, p. 15)

It will be seen that the subject is aware that the leaves which he seems to be seeing do not have the status of real leaves, and he is lucid enough to ascribe the whole experience to the abnormal functioning of his own brain due to intoxication by the drug.

Where we would take issue with the writer is over his description of the experience as a 'partial hallucination'. As we have attempted to show above, there are considerable theoretical difficulties in the concept of a hallucination which only occupies part of the visual field, the rest being taken up by normal perception. We think for this reason that it is desirable to consider the metachoric hypothesis even in a case such as this, in which the subject believes himself to be perceiving most of the environment normally. In other words, we would suggest that Professor Price may have been hallucinating the whole scene, and not just the leaves on the bedspread, even though most of that scene corresponded closely, or so at any rate he believed, to his real physical environment at the time.

If this interpretation of the experience is correct, it makes it appear more similar to a lucid dream initiated from sleep than might otherwise have seemed to be the case. The subject, on this view, is examining his totally hallucinatory environment in a detached but interested manner very similar to that often adopted by lucid dreamers.

CONCLUSION

We arrive, then, at the somewhat surprising conclusion that people are, in general, considerably more liable to a completely hallucinatory perceptual experience than has previously been recognised. Even if these experiences, or some types of them, tend to occur to people with certain personality characteristics, or to people who may be mentally ill as well as to those who are not, it seems clear that these experiences happen to, or could be developed by, a very significant cross-section of the ostensibly normal population, that is to say, people who are living in a functional way and who do not have any particular psychiatric history.

In the next chapters we will consider in more detail two of the types of metachoric experience which we have mentioned – false awakenings and out-of-the-body experiences – and their relationships to lucid dreams. We will find that these phenomena lend weight to the idea, suggested by lucid dreams themselves, that hallucinatory experiences in normal subjects are capable of displaying both a high degree of perceptual realism and a surprisingly high level of rationality on the part of the subject.

Chapter 7

False awakenings and out-of-the-body experiences

REPEATED FALSE AWAKENINGS

False awakenings are a type of metachoric or hallucinatory experience which may occur even to people who have not had lucid dreams, but which someone who does experience frequent lucid dreams seems particularly prone to have. They can take a number of distinct forms, but in all of these a person believes that he has woken up when he has not. Thus the dreamer may appear to awake realistically in his own bedroom and finds his room, which may seem to be familiar in all its details, around him; and if he does not realise that he is dreaming, a more or less plausible representation of the process of dressing, breakfasting and setting off to work may then follow. The essential difference between a false awakening and a lucid dream, therefore, lies in the fact that during a false awakening the subject lacks insight into his or her condition. In other respects false awakenings may resemble lucid dreams fairly closely. In particular, the perceptual quality of the experience may appear to mimic very realistically that of waking life.

One of the most dramatic forms of false awakening is that in which the person seems to awaken repeatedly, but without actually doing so. Some subjects report waking up in their bedrooms several times in succession, and seemingly setting off for work and beginning their normal day each time, before being aroused to apparent wakefulness by some discrepancy in the dream content and finding themselves back in their bedroom thinking, 'Oh, that was a dream'. The following is an example of this type of experience, reported by a French psychologist, Yves Delage:

This happened when I was in the Roscoff laboratory. One night, I was woken by urgent knocking at the door of my room. I got up and asked: 'Who is there?' 'Monsieur,' came the answer in the voice of Marty (the laboratory caretaker), 'it is Madame H——' (someone who was really living in the town at that time and was among my acquaintances), 'who is asking you to come immediately to her house to see Mademoiselle P——' (someone who was really part of Madame H's household and who was also known to me), 'who has suddenly fallen ill.'

'Just give me time to dress,' I said, 'and I will run.' I dressed hurriedly, but before going out I went into my dressing-room to wipe my face with a damp sponge. The sensation of cold water woke me and I realised that I had dreamt all the foregoing events and that no one had come to ask for me. So I went back and to sleep. But a little later, the same knocking came again at my door. 'What, Monsieur, aren't you coming then?'

'Good heavens! So it really is true, I thought I had dreamt it.'

'Not at all. Hurry up. They are all waiting for you.'

'All right, I will run.' Again I dressed myself, again in my dressing-room I wiped my face with cold water, and again the sensation of the cold water woke me and made me understand that I had been deceived by a repetition of my dream. I went back to bed and went to sleep again.

The same scene re-enacted itself almost identically twice more. In the morning, when I really awoke, I could see from the full water jug, the empty bowl, and the dry sponge, that all this had been really a dream; not only the knockings at my door and the conversations with the caretaker, but having dressed, having been in my dressing-room, having washed my face, having believed that I woke up after the dream and having gone back to bed. This whole series of actions, reasonings and thoughts had been nothing but a dream repeated four times in succession with no break in my sleep and without my having stirred from my bed.

(Delage, 1919, pp. 451–1)

The philosopher Bertrand Russell, interestingly, reports appearing to wake up hundreds of times in succession after an anaesthetic (Russell, 1948, p. 186).

REALISM AND UNREALISM IN FALSE AWAKENINGS

The Delage example quoted above may be taken as illustrating the point that false awakenings, like pre-lucid dreams, tend to resemble lucid dreams more than non-lucid ones. For example, the environment often appears to be meticulously realistic and the dreamer in a fairly rational state of mind. On the other hand, the defining factor of lucidity – awareness of the status of the experience – is clearly lacking in a false awakening. This absence may be linked to a more general lack of criticalness in the state. For example, the subject of a false awakening is often strangely naïve about the observations that would genuinely support the conclusion that they have come awake. Thus it is quite common for a person in a pre-lucid or lucid dream state to suddenly acquire the belief, as Delage did, that he is now awake, although previously he was dreaming. In other words, a lucid dreamer may be wandering around an unfamiliar environment in his dream when something happens that causes him to believe that he has 'come awake', although all that really happens is that he proceeds to have a further sequence of dream experiences in the same environment, only now they are non-lucid. An example of this kind, reported by Subject C, has been quoted on p. 54.

The false awakening quoted above was unrealistic in the sense that the subject appeared to wake, not in the bedroom in which he was sleeping at the time, but in a place (his old school) in which the preceding lucid dream had been set. Further, the subject considered on waking that the experience following the false awakening was phenomenologically indistinguishable from an ordinary dream. It is curious that it does not occur to the subject in this situation that he has not gone through the usual transition of awakening in his bed, between what he now regards retrospectively as a dream, and his current, supposedly wakeful state.

False awakenings may be categorised as realistic or unrealistic, not only with respect to whether a plausible process of apparent 'waking up' takes place within the dream narrative, but also with respect to whether the subject seems to find himself in his own bedroom (or wherever he is sleeping at the time) once the false awakening has started. In the following experience of Moers-Messmer, the subject goes through an apparently realistic process of 'waking up' at the start, but he then finds himself in a room which is not that which he is currently occupying (although this does not occur to him at the time):

> I awaken in bed and look around myself. It is already light, I find myself in a room in which I lived as a child twenty years ago, but I do not realise this. But something else strikes me instead; I hear voices and sounds, which seem to be coming from all directions. I think that this is sure to be an after-effect of sleep, and that I now have the opportunity to write down word by word what the voices are saying. All at once I find a pencil in my hand and see a notepad lying on the bed in front of me. This makes me suspicious. I think: If I did not pick up a pencil, then it should not be in my hand, and if it is there, there must be something wrong with me. The most plausible explanation would be to regard it as a dream, if I had not just woken up. *So, I think, now for the first time I am really awake.* Only the voices, which I still hear, worry me. For it occurs to me that hallucinations in a waking state are a sure sign of mental disturbance. I get up and begin to search. When I open the door of the bedside table, I see inside it the parts of a radio piled up: tubes, transformers, and coils; in addition to a loudspeaker funnel there is a small glowing light-bulb. I pull a connection out of the accumulator, upon which the tubes go out, but the light-bulb goes on burning. At the same moment the voices and sounds also vanish. But immediately afterwards they start again, at first softly, then becoming continually louder, and music joins in. Now I give up the struggle and think: I hope that no one will notice that I am out of my mind – and I continue to dream.
>
> (Moers-Messmer, 1938; our italics)

These two sorts of unrealism – that with regard to the absence of a simulated process of 'waking up' and that concerning the environment into which the subject seems to wake – do not necessarily occur together in every case, as the Delage case quoted above may illustrate. Delage finds himself in his proper bedroom each time, but he appears not to have gone through any realistic process of 'waking' at any stage; instead, each time he 'wakes' at his washstand and then decides to 'go back to bed', without it apparently occurring to him how implausible it is that he should wake up at the washstand, following an episode, not of unconscious sleepwalking, say, but one of apparently waking consciousness.

TYPE 2 FALSE AWAKENINGS

A particularly striking kind of realistic false awakening was distinguished in Green's book *Lucid Dreams* (1968a) as a 'Type 2' false awakening. In such an experience the subject seems to wake in his or her bed in the normal way, but the atmosphere seems stressed, electrified or tense, and he or she has a feeling of foreboding or expectancy. In a false awakening of this kind ominous and anxiety-producing noises may be heard, and 'apparitions' may be seen; that is, strange figures incongruous with the bedroom or whatever other environment the subject happens to be sleeping in.

The Type 2 false awakening seems to be one of the less consistently pleasant types of metachoric experience, in view of the sensations of tension and electricity in the atmosphere which are often reported, together with the feelings of expectation, which may be apprehensive or oppressively ominous. The following is an experience reported by Subject E in which 'apparitions' of monsters were perceived.

> I awoke to the realisation that the bedside radio was still on. Someone passed the door on the way downstairs. I turned the music low; strange, I thought, the radio being on at this time of night – what *was* the time? I reached out of bed to look at the clock (about six feet away) but as I did so an eerie feeling came over me, and I hesitated; yet everything looked perfectly natural so I went ahead, against a mounting tension of the atmosphere, and picked up the clock – hereupon it suddenly changed in my hands! Hastily I put it down; its black dial had turned white and hands moved to the nine and ten. I recognised this was the false awakening. Pausing a moment to ponder the significance of the position of the hands (for I knew this could not represent the actual time) I dived back under the blankets. Monsters were pressing on me, I called for help but could not wake up – not until I had seized the monsters and fought them, and flung them on the floor.

It is interesting to note, in view of our argument in Chapter 6 that there is a close relationship between the various types of fully hallucinatory experience, that some subjects have claimed that if one finds oneself in a false awakening of this type and manages to recognise it as such, one may be able to enter a particularly interesting kind of lucid dream or out-of-the-body experience. Oliver Fox, for example, claimed that once one was in this state it was only necessary to get up from one's bed with the deliberate intention of entering an ecsomatic experience and one would be able to look back on one's body lying in the bed behind one. The association of false awakenings with out-of-the-body experiences and phenomena analogous to apparitions occurring in the waking state is another indication of the close relationship between these different types of experience.

The following is one of Oliver Fox's experiences of the Type 2 false awakening.

> I passed from unremembered dreams and thought I was awake. It was still night, and my room very dark. Although it seemed to me that I was awake, I felt curiously disinclined to move. The atmosphere seemed charged, to be in a 'strained' condition. I had a sense of invisible, intangible powers at work, which caused this feeling of aerial stress. I became expectant. Certainly something was about to happen. Suddenly the room was faintly illuminated. A soft greenish glow, suggesting phosphorescence, was emanating from a glass-doored Japanese cabinet beside my bed. From this source it spread slowly and evenly, like a luminous gas – a cold, spectral light, of unvarying brightness. For a while I stayed motionless, watching it. I did not feel afraid, but I was filled with wonder. Then, wishing to observe more closely the source of this mysterious light, I made an effort to overcome my strange disinclination to move. Instantly the light vanished and things were as usual. I was really awake now, with my head half raised from the pillow.
>
> (Fox, 1962, p. 48)

It is interesting to note that Fox refers to feeling 'curiously disinclined to move' at the start of this experience, and that he relates its ending to his eventually overcoming this reluctance. It is possible that, had he tried to move, he would have found himself unable to do so, since paralysis is sometimes reported as a feature of the Type 2 false awakening (see, for example, Subject E's remarks quoted on pp. 97–8). We shall discuss the significance of this finding further in Chapter 8, in connection with the possible relationship between Type 2 false awakenings and the disorder which clinicians call 'sleep paralysis', in which the subject seems to wake up but is unable to move, and in connection with which hallucinations may be reported. In the mean time we would draw attention to the possibility that the monsters which appeared to 'press' on Subject E in the preceding case may also have been related to lowered muscle tone, and may have been a symbolic representation of a difficulty in breathing. Chodoff (1944), describing a case of sleep paralysis in a 19-year-old staff sergeant in the US army, mentions an occasion on which the young man seemed to wake up only to experience 'the vivid hallucination that a friend was sitting on his chest'. Chodoff suggests that this hallucination was triggered by the subject experiencing difficulty in breathing, and that the 'consequent feeling of substernal oppression was misinterpreted as someone sitting on his chest'.

OUT-OF-THE-BODY EXPERIENCES

In this section we will consider a type of experience which is closely related to the lucid dream. This is the out-of-the-body experience (OBE). As an alternative to the rather cumbrous adjective 'out-of-the-body', Green (1968b) proposed the term 'ecsomatic', and we make use of both terms in this book. These terms are meant to be purely descriptive, and no particular connotation is intended with regard to the theoretical interpretation of such experiences.

Ecsomatic experiences present us with an anomaly which is in some ways similar to that presented by lucid dreams themselves, in that both these types of experience appear to be a fairly constant part of human experience, accessible to a significant proportion of the population, and have probably been so throughout recorded history. In spite of this, and in spite of their striking and paradoxical nature, they have remained until quite recently unrecognised as identifiable phenomena.

The most typical kind of out-of-the-body experience is that in which the subject apparently changes his point of view and finds himself surveying his environment and even his own physical body as if from the outside. OBEs were, before our first public appeal for cases in 1966, perhaps slightly more recognised as a phenomenon in their own right than were lucid dreams. However, this recognition was confined to a limited class of people; that is, people who had spiritualist or occult beliefs of some kind, and who found their beliefs reinforced by ideas concerning an 'astral body' or similar concepts. This state of affairs had the result that those outside the very limited circle of people who were able to integrate ideas of an astral body into their models of human existence regarded the production of stories concerning such things as the result of fantastic imagining if not outright invention and took little interest in them, if they had heard of them at all.

Since our first appeal for cases it has gradually emerged that the situation is really quite different from what had largely been supposed. OBEs are experienced by a cross-section of the normal population, including people who have little perceptible tendency to interest themselves in surprising experiences or theories of the spiritualistic type. Not only do they happen to people who have no interest or expectation in this direction, but they also happen in a wide variety of circumstances. Although there is a class of OBE which seems to be triggered by stress, for example when the subject is in a life-threatening situation, a large number of OBEs occur when there is no obvious predisposing factor involved.

One respect, however, in which OBEs differ from lucid dreams, and which may perhaps make their neglect less surprising, is that they do not appear to be very susceptible to training or development. It seems that a small minority of people find it possible to have OBEs frequently, and to some extent at their own volition. Much more commonly, however, a person may have one, or perhaps two, of these surprising experiences in a lifetime. Even if the experiences arouse the curiosity of such individuals, there is little they can do to repeat them.

We shall start by considering the most typical form of ecsomatic experience and lucid dream, and the relationships and differences between them. There are, as we shall see, intermediate experiences which can be classified about as easily one way as the other, but the most typical experience in each category is quite distinct and there is no risk of confusing these two forms.

We have already given a number of characteristic examples of lucid dreams in previous chapters. We have seen that a lucid dream is an experience that occurs during sleep, and that the subject finds himself in an environment which may appear to be completely realistic, but which he is usually in no danger of confusing with his real environment because the typical lucid dream does not appear to be continuous with his waking experience, or to be providing him with a view of the bedroom in which he is sleeping.

The typical out-of-the-body experience, by contrast, starts from a waking state, and the subject usually has the impression that the perceptual environment is identical with his or her actual environment. It is probably this which helped give rise to the spiritualistic interpretation of OBEs. According to the 'astral body' theory of spiritualists, there is enclosed within the normal physical body an identical, spiritual one which perceptually functions in the same way as the physical one, so that when it moves out of co-ordination with the physical one, the same environment is being perceived, although from a different point of view.

One of the differences between the typical out-of-the-body experience and the typical lucid dream is that the subject of an OBE will often not perceive a hallucinatory 'body image'. They may be said to have an identification with a specific area of the perceptual environment in the sense of seeming to see their physical bodies from some particular point of view, but they do not necessarily seem to themselves to have a duplicate body of a similar appearance to their real body. Whereas the lucid dreamer almost invariably seems to have a physical body of the normal human kind, and most likely one which he accepts as having an appearance identical with that of his actual body, an OBE subject will on occasion seem to have such a body, but may also find himself identified with a vague cloud or blur, or indeed with nothing more than a point of view from which an apparently seeing eye is operating.

The following case illustrates one of the possible variants. In this instance the subject sees her normal body 'left behind' on the bed, but appears to lack a 'duplicate' body, although it is not clear whether she would also have failed to see a duplicate body if she had 'looked down' rather than used a mirror.

> I went to my room and lay on my bed. . . . After a while my whole body felt very heavy and sank into the bed. I tried to get up but could not. Then I found I was standing in front of the dressing-table mirror. I looked into it, there was no reflection of me. I touched the mirror to make sure it was there. It was, but I was not, but I could see across the room in the mirror. I was still lying on my bed. This time I became terrified.

Frantically I wondered how to get back in! . . . I went back to
the bed, lay with my body.

(Green, 1986b, pp. 73–4)

In lucid dreams it is rare, indeed virtually unknown, for the dreamer
to be identified with an apparently incorporeal point of view, or
with anything which differs significantly from his normal waking
physical body. That is to say, he or she seems to have a normal body
which produces the various expected visual and other sensations.
Typically, this body image appears to be the same as his or her
normal waking one. However, there are a few cases in which lucid
dreamers have atypical or unrealistic body images. People may, for
example, have lucid dreams in which they are different people or
people of the opposite sex. The following is a dream reported by
J. H. M. Whiteman in which he dreamed that he was a girl.

Awareness in separation began with the sight of a tree, about
twenty feet away, in a pleasant natural scene. I moved a little
nearer, so that the tree was on my left. The freshness of the air
and the joy of being in a smaller and acceptable form again
made me start dancing, with movements exhilarating in their
freedom. . . . Still affected with the joy in nature, I lay down on
the ground, vividly feeling the cool grass with my fingers and
the firmness of the earth beneath. I began to be afraid of the
mounting excitement, that it would pass beyond my control,
and decided to stand up again. As I did so, I noticed vividly
how different it was, getting up off the ground in my proper
form, from what it would have been in my physical body, on
account of the great differences in bodily form, the smaller
height, and the proportionately wider hips. In spite of this
being, as it were, a strange discovery, the movement was
completely natural to me, and wonderfully satisfying in its
ease and grace. The memory-impression of what the contrasting movements of my physical body would have been, on
the other hand, seemed only an outer illusory and provisional
covering to the reality I was experiencing.

(Whiteman, 1961, p. 186)

'INTERMEDIATE' EXPERIENCES

From the point of view of the metachoric model of hallucination
put forward in the preceding chapter, it is of interest that there

appears to be a set of experiences midway between lucid dreams and OBEs, which are difficult to classify unambiguously one way rather than the other.

Oliver Fox, for example, believed that if he prolonged his lucid dreams by an effort of will there would come a point at which a definite 'click' was experienced and he would find himself in an ecsomatic state (Fox, 1962). Like most of the habitual experiencers of states resembling an OBE and also of states resembling a lucid dream, he classified the former as more vivid, more significant and more emotionally charged. We see therefore that in the class of experiences occurring to habitual ecsomatic experience subjects (who are also often habitual lucid dream subjects) there seems to be a fairly close relationship between the two types of experience.

Furthermore, in spite of the differences between the most typical forms of each class of experience, we see that they are both experiences in which the subject is perceiving a completely hallucinatory environment, which may seem to be as realistic and detailed as the normal physical world, and which he or she is perceiving from a distinct point of view that in both cases may be associated with an alternative body image, although in the case of lucid dreams this is far more likely to be a fairly accurate reproduction of the normal one.

Certainly it is possible to find cases drawn from the two different categories which exhibit a striking resemblance to each other in many respects, such as the subject's sense of freedom or liberation, his exploratory attitude towards his situation, and its strikingly detailed and vivid realism.

One of the obvious differences between out-of-the-body experiences and lucid dreams concerns the subject's degree of insight in the sense of his or her awareness of the situation. As previously discussed, a lucid dreamer, by our definition, must have insight, since his state is determined by his awareness that he is dreaming; whereas the subject of an OBE may or may not be aware of the hallucinatory nature of his experience. Most people who have had a large number of lucid dreams and ecsomatic experiences regard the latter as the superior type of experience, in that they provide them with a greater sense of reality and vividness. However, in one respect the lucid dreamer is in a more realistic frame of mind than the typical OBE subject, since the lucid dreamer is not usually under any temptation to confuse the experience with waking life. By contrast, the OBE subject may believe that he is observing the world of normal life, and fail to draw the conclusion that, however closely it resembles normal life, it is actually a hallucinatory representation of it.

However, in many ways, and particularly in certain types of experience, this seems a very pardonable assumption. The OBE subject may seem to be seeing something which gives him or her information about the world in much the same way as do perceptions of the physical world.

Moreover, since there is a tendency, even among people (in a normal state of consciousness) who are studying reports of OBEs, to believe that they might be cases of actual perception from a different point of view, and not hallucinations, it would seem somewhat harsh to say that an OBE subject is showing defective insight in failing to come to the correct conclusion himself.

CONCLUSION

To conclude this chapter, Table 7.1 attempts to show in summary form some of the similarities and differences between the various

Table 7.1 Some characteristics of different metachoric experiences

	Lucid dream	False awakening	OBE	Apparition	Waking dream
Insight	complete	no	usually	usually by the end of the experience	sometimes not for long periods
Continuity with previous waking experience	no	no	can be complete	usually complete	can be complete
Time-scale	1–6 mins	up to a few mins	up to a few mins	up to a few mins	up to half an hour (?)
Emotions	neutral to elated	negative	can be very positive	neutral to negative	neutral (?)
Realism (imitation of reality)	variable	variable	usually very good	usually very good	very good (?)

Source: Adapted from Green, 1990

hallucinatory states we have been discussing. There are a number of points worth bringing out in connection with this table. First, by 'insight' we mean only that the subject is aware that something anomalous is going on perceptually, not that he or she interprets this anomaly in any particular way. As we discussed in the context of subjects' intellectual functioning in lucid dreams, the subjects of OBEs and apparitional experiences may realise something anomalous is happening without necessarily concluding that they are hallucinating. Indeed, such an interpretation seems to be the exception rather than the rule, as we indicated above.

Secondly, with regard to 'continuity with previous waking experience', it is interesting to note that even false awakenings, which begin with an apparent 'waking' from sleep, can mimic normal experience in that the discontinuity which occurs at the start is one which we all experience normally every time we actually wake up. Moreover, OBEs, apparitions and waking dreams can all be experienced as seamlessly integrated into previous waking experience to an extent which justifies, and may help to explain, the slowness with which the subject may achieve insight.

A final point to which we would draw attention is that when we come to consider the time-scale of the various metachoric experiences, waking dreams seem to differ from the others. The other categories seem to be fairly standardised at not more than a few minutes in length, whereas waking dreams seem able to extend for as much as half an hour (at least, for half an hour of subjective experience) and possibly longer. (See Green, 1990, for a discussion of some ostensible examples of this phenomenon.) This would seem to make them possible candidates to explain the relatively long and complex 'sightings' of UFOs (unidentified flying objects) which are sometimes reported.

In Chapter 8 we will put forward some empirical and theoretical considerations which we think strengthen the case for a degree of continuity between the various states represented in Table 7.1.

Chapter 8

Paralysis in hallucinatory states

Paralysis is a feature which is occasionally reported in connection with a number of different types of isolated hallucinatory experience occurring to normal people. It has been reported in connection with all the hallucinatory states we have been considering in Chapters 6 and 7; that is, lucid dreams, false awakenings, out-of-the-body experiences and apparitions. We think a consideration of this feature strengthens the case for a certain degree of continuity between the various states, and has the potential to shed light on the relationship between these experiences and the ordinary sleep state. In this chapter we shall discuss some cases of each type of experience, all of which include paralysis as a feature, and present some theoretical arguments for the idea that sleep processes may underlie all of these states, even those ostensibly starting from and ending in the waking state.

LUCID DREAMS, FALSE AWAKENINGS AND SLEEP PARALYSIS

In our discussion of the possibility of claustrophobia in lucid dreams (p. 48) we quoted an example occurring in a child in which the claustrophobia was related to attempts to wake up which were not immediately successful. The following is a rather similar report provided by an adult subject, a psychologist. In this case the claustrophobia is directly related by the subject to his inability to move.

> Ever since I was about 14 I have had various experiences connected with realising when I was dreaming. These have

been quite spontaneous but fairly irregular. The experiences involve either (a) controlling the dream; or (b) trying to wake up . . . .

In experiences of the second type (trying to wake up), I would realise that I was dreaming, but decide dreaming wasn't enough and I would get a strong desire to be able to move my actual limbs. My limbs, however, would remain motionless despite efforts to move them. This would make me feel very claustrophobic and my efforts to move would intensify. It was an effort to maintain awareness of my actual body, but for some reason I was afraid that if I stopped trying to move I would get wrapped up in the dream and remain paralysed. Usually I found that I could at least twitch a finger (I could also control rate of breathing). I would then try and twitch it again and build up the motion. Eventually I would produce a large enough motion and wake up.

A notable feature of this case is the fact that the experiences seem to be associated with the hypnopompic state. In this respect they resemble Type 2 false awakenings, and we have already seen in Chapter 7 how paralysis may be associated with the latter type of hallucinatory experience. In this connection it may be relevant to note that periods of REM sleep, with their combination of lowered muscle tone and heightened cortical arousal, tend to become more frequent and prolonged as the night progresses.

A feature of Type 2 false awakenings is that it characteristically takes the subject some time, if not several occurrences of this type of experience, for him to be able to recognise a Type 2 false awakening as a hallucinatory state distinct from waking experience. He may eventually come to this recognition, either because the 'atmosphere' of his false awakening is unrealistic in some way (for example, seeming 'tense' or 'charged'), or because he experiences 'apparitional' effects when in the state. Characteristically he seems to wake in his bedroom, and this is no doubt part of the reason for the subject's initially being confused about whether he is awake or asleep, despite what may be in other respects a relatively high degree of cognitive functionality when compared with non-lucid sleep.

It is interesting to compare the phenomenon of the Type 2 false awakening with the disorder of sleep paralysis. It is possible that the two classes of experience may overlap to some extent. Some

of the differences between the accounts of Type 2 false
awakenings which we have received and the experiences
described in the literature of sleep paralysis may to some extent
be due to the different methods of subject recruitment in the two
cases. The subjects referred to in the literature of sleep paralysis
are usually 'patients' who have come to the attention of
physicians, either directly by reason of the suffering or
dysfunctionality caused by the episodes of sleep paralysis, or
indirectly because of some other form of pathology. Our own
subjects, on the other hand, have usually been healthy people
who encountered the Type 2 false awakening apparently as an
incidental by-product, albeit sometimes a disagreeable one, of
their cultivation of lucid dreams and/or ecsomatic experiences.

To illustrate the phenomenological similarity between the
types of experience which are reported in the two contexts, sleep
paralysis and Type 2 false awakening, we will quote a case from
Schneck (1957). It is unfortunately not in the subject's own words,
but is presumably based on the author's contemporaneous case
notes. The subject was a 51-year-old woman, and the following
experience apparently happened three times, widely spaced over
a year, and was similar on each occasion.

> She was asleep and suddenly felt that the mattress had moved.
> It was as if someone had been sitting on it and had then stood
> up. The patient became fully aware of her home surroundings
> but was unable to move her body. Her eyes were closed and
> she was terrified. She then experienced an hallucination of
> someone walking around the room. Muscle tenseness accom-
> panied her feeling of anxiety. She had the impression that a
> long time was passing. She was afraid to see who this person
> might be. After some time the patient sat up suddenly and
> opened her eyes. Her fear gradually subsided. Despite her
> paralysis and fear, the patient had the impression that the
> hallucinated figure was a woman whose interest in her was
> kindly, helpful and sympathetic, especially in relation to the
> problems the patient had experienced in her lifetime. The pro-
> tective aura reminded the patient of a mother-like person and
> association was with her own mother who had died when the
> patient was 2 years old. This association intensified her fear.

It is unfortunate that there are ambiguities in this account that
might have been resolved if it had been in the first person. The

chief of these from the present point of view concerns the similarity or otherwise of the quasi-sensory part of the experience to normal perception. The description of the subject as becoming 'fully aware of her home surroundings' could mean either that she was cognitively aware that she was in her bedroom or that she actually had a realistic 'perception' of her bedroom around her. If the latter interpretation is the correct one, then the experience could be described as a metachoric one, i.e. one in which the subject's entire perceptual environment was hallucinatory, since it is said that her eyes were closed at this stage. Similarly, the phrase 'she then experienced an hallucination of someone walking around the room' could imply either an experience closely imitating normal perception, or merely a 'sense of presence' without any quasi-perceptual content (for examples of the latter, see Green and McCreery, 1975). The negative emotional tone of the experience and the tactile hallucination of the mattress moving would both be characteristic of a Type 2 false awakening.

In other cases it is claimed the subject's eyes have been open during attacks of sleep paralysis. Levin (1933) describes a woman of 21 who was subject to 'frequent' attacks, during which she experienced both auditory hallucinations (for example, of her father talking) and visual ones (apparently of the people heard). He reports that 'at times the eyelids were uninvolved in the paralysis, so that the patient opened her eyes but was unable otherwise to move'; also that the visual hallucinations of people occurred 'with her eyes open' (p. 4). However, it seems likely that this patient was only seen by Levin in the clinical setting and not at home while the attacks occurred, so it would appear that we have only the subject's impression that her eyes were open as evidence that they were. We would suggest that in at least some cases like this the subject may be mistaken and his or her eyes may actually remain shut throughout, as they presumably did throughout the experiences of Fox and Subject E quoted on pp. 69–70. There would seem no reason in principle why someone should not hallucinate the tactile and proprioceptive sensations appropriate to opening and keeping open the eyes at the same time as experiencing visual and/or auditory hallucinations of people in the bedroom.

It is worth noting that even in the literature of sleep paralysis it is recognised that such episodes are not always to be regarded as symptomatic of a long-standing disorder, but may occur relatively infrequently in a given individual. Schneck (1957), for example, suggests that the phenomenon may be more widespread than has been generally realised, because subjects in whom it is an infrequent occurrence may never report it to a physician. Parkes (1985) concludes on the basis of several different studies that episodes occur at least once in a lifetime in up to 40-50 per cent of all normal subjects. In some cases sleep paralysis seems to be triggered by, or at any rate to immediately follow, a nightmare or a highly stressful dream (Chodoff, 1944).

On the other hand, not all cases of sleep paralysis share an apparent perception or awareness of the sleeper's surroundings with Type 2 false awakenings. Max Levin, for example, who himself suffered from attacks 'several times a year', described his own experiences as follows:

> In the attack I know I am in bed but am otherwise not aware of my surroundings. My eyes are closed. I am conscious of complete inability to move, except to breathe. Breathing seems to be labored, so that I have the idea (during the attack) that the blanket is over my mouth, but can do nothing about it. There is extreme discomfort and anxiety. Though I have been interested in sleep paralysis for years and was the first to employ this phrase in the title of an article, never yet has the thought flashed through my mind, 'This is only an attack of sleep paralysis; I must have patience, it will soon pass.' I seem to hope that relief will come with the next breath, but each breath leaves me still paralyzed. Finally, after half a dozen unsuccessful attempts, on the next breath I feel as if I am making a Herculean effort, and immediately the spell is broken and I am wide awake and in full possession of my faculties.
>
> (Levin, 1957)

Parkes (1985) likens the physiology of sleep paralysis attacks to that of REM sleep. He writes: 'The generalized reduction of muscle tone, preservation of eye movements, and depression or loss of spinal reflexes of sleep paralysis are mirrored during REM sleep.' However, he seems reluctant to conclude that the subject's state in a sleep paralysis attack is fully that of sleep, since elsewhere he writes: 'During sleep paralysis, there is partial or complete flaccid paralysis of skeletal, but not extra-ocular muscles with areflexia [absence of spinal reflexes], similar to the findings during REM sleep, although the patient is awake.' On the other hand, in another place he concedes that 'sleep paralysis . . . appears to be a form of dissociated REM sleep.'

One reason why clinical writers such as Parkes may doubt that the subject of a sleep paralysis attack is really asleep is the fact that the subject is ostensibly aware of his physical surroundings. For example, Parkes (1985) writes: 'EEG recordings in patients during sleep paralysis are normal except for the pattern of light sleep during conscious awareness.' This combination may seem less baffling if we consider that the perceptual environment during these attacks may be entirely hallucinatory, i.e. metachoric, even if it faithfully mimics the subject's real environment at the time. In this respect these cases would be no different from out-of-the-body experiences, in which the subject ostensibly 'sees' a more or less exact hallucinatory replica of the room in which he or she is situated at the time, but from a perspective which is inappropriate to the position of his or her physical body.

The question here is clearly in part semantic, namely how should we define 'sleep'? Sleep is usually characterised by such features as reduced muscle tone, relatively low cortical arousal, poor cognitive functioning, and lack of responsiveness to external stimuli. On a more global level, and partly arising out of these features, we do not normally expect a sleeper to be aware of his physical surroundings, or the position of his physical body, or to be capable of communication with someone who is awake. However, in anomalous states such as lucid dreaming, false awakenings, and possibly sleep paralysis, we find some of the normal features of sleep present but not others. If we adopt a definition of sleep which requires all the normal features to be present at all times, then we might be forced to describe the subjects of lucid dreams and false awakenings as awake. This seems counter-intuitive in the light of some of the features which are present in such states, such as the EEG and other electro-physiological accompaniments of lucid dreams which appear to be similar to those of non-lucid REM sleep. We think it is more helpful to continue to regard the subjects of these anomalous states as asleep, but to recognise that 'sleep' is a complex concept with even more variants than has been recognised hitherto.

To conclude this section, Type 2 false awakenings and the

phenomenon of sleep paralysis seem to represent, like REM sleep, a 'paradoxical' combination of extreme muscular inhibition with relative cortical excitation. We shall be discussing the theoretical significance of this fact in relation to the question of individual differences in propensity for lucid dreaming in Chapter 15 of this book. In the following section, we consider cases of paralysis occurring in connection with out-of-the-body experiences.

PARALYSIS AND OUT-OF-THE-BODY EXPERIENCES

Green (1968b) found that nearly 5 per cent of a population of 400 subjects who had had out-of-the-body experiences reported paralysis at some stage of their experience. The paralysis could occur before, during or after the ecsomatic state. The following is an example of paralysis beginning before the initiation of the ecsomatic hallucination proper:

> I was lying on top of my bed after a two hour sleep. . . . I had woken up, but could not move or even open my eyes . . . then I remember a dreadful noise came into my head so loud it was deafening, then a very loud popping noise came from my head and I seemed to shoot out of my head, and went up in the air, then turned round and looked down at my self fully clothed lying on top of the bed.
>
> (Green, 1968b, p. 60)

The case just quoted may be regarded as a hypnopompic one, reminiscent in some ways of the cases of sleep paralysis described above. However, it is interesting to note that the subject may report paralysis accompanying OBEs in other situations. The following case is one in which there were recurrent experiences of paralysis and OBEs, apparently in the hypnagogic state. Paralysis seems to have been an invariable precursor of the ecsomatic state in this case, though in others we have received the subject apparently experienced paralysis on some occasions but not on others.

> I would lie in bed reading, and then quite suddenly I would have the physical experience of becoming stiff. I would try to move, but the experience was so unpleasant that I felt if I relaxed I would be able to come out of this (whatever it was)

more quickly, however by doing this I found that I appeared to be floating around, I could see myself lying in bed reading . . . then I would again suddenly be able to move.

(Green, 1968b, pp. 61–2)

It seems possible that in some cases paralysis might in principle be present without the subject noticing it. That is to say, there might be subjects who would have found themselves unable to move during the ecsomatic state had they tried to do so, and who failed to notice their inability simply because they did not try to execute any voluntary movements. This hypothesis might apply particularly to the relatively large number of subjects to whom the out-of-the-body experience occurs while lying down. If there is any truth in this idea, then the figure of under 5 per cent for cases in which paralysis is reported to occur might actually under-represent the proportion of cases in which paralysis is actually present.

However, we must recognise that the hypothesis of undetected paralysis could not apply to all reported cases, since in many of them the subject is allegedly in motion at the time of the experience, for example, walking, or even performing some relatively skilled perceptual-motor task such as riding a motor-cycle. To account for this fact we will have recourse to a model of out-of-the-body experiences put forward by McCreery (1994), according to which an OBE subject is in a state of sleep during the course of the OBE, even if he is highly aroused immediately prior to the start of the experience.

It has been noted, for example by Irwin (1985), that OBEs seem to occur at extremes of cortical arousal, whether high or low. As regards the low end of the scale, we found that three-quarters of our subjects reporting only one OBE in their lifetime were lying down at the time, and 12 per cent thought they were actually asleep immediately prior to the start of the experience (Green, 1968b). By contrast some OBEs are reported to occur during such situations as rock-climbing falls, car accidents, childbirth and job interviews.

McCreery's (1994) hypothesis is that the former group remain asleep throughout the OBE state, and that the latter group are also temporarily asleep, however paradoxical this may appear at first sight. Oswald (1962) has drawn attention to the fact that sleep can supervene on extreme stress as well as the more normal state of relaxation, de-afferentation (lack of sensory input) and low general arousal. The evidence for this is both anecdotal and experimental. On the experimental level, Oswald (1959) was able to induce sleep in four out of a group of six volunteer subjects by administering 'powerful' shocks at regular ten-second intervals to the wrist or ankle of the subject. On the anecdotal level, Oswald alludes to cases such as those of soldiers falling asleep while waiting to go into battle, or of people falling asleep while waiting to give an important public address. He devotes a chapter to what he calls 'sleep as a provoked response', under which heading he includes 'those times when a sleep state results from overwhelming or terrifying stimulation' (1962, p. 30). Overwhelming or terrifying stimulation would seem a good characterisation of many of the situations in which high-arousal OBEs occur, such as the following:

> My ex-husband and I had a row in which he tried to strangle me. . . . I seemed to float above my body and could see myself slowly slide down the wall. Everything seemed to be in slow motion, but also I had this very beautiful serene feeling. . . . The next thing I knew, I was waking up lying on the floor.

It might be objected that OBE subjects sometimes report ecsomatic experiences as having occurred while they performed complex motor tasks, such as driving cars, playing musical instruments or delivering speeches. However, two considerations may be relevant here. First, the perceptual-motor skills in question are usually highly practised and habitual ones, and there is both anecdotal and laboratory evidence that people who are cortically, but not behaviourally, asleep can perform complex perceptual-motor tasks of this sort. On the anecdotal level for example, there is evidence of soldiers sleeping while on the march, and in the laboratory it has been confirmed that people can carry out quite complex behaviours while sleep-walking. Sleep-walking has been found to be associated with non-REM stages of sleep known as 'slow-wave sleep' (SWS) because of the predominance in them of slow irregular *delta* waves of 1-3 cycles a second (Parkes, 1985).

Secondly, the experiences in question may not last as long in reality as the subject thinks they do. It is known that the sense of time can be distorted in hypnagogic states, and the same may be true of OBEs if they are indeed a phenomenon of sleep. It is interesting to note that 17 per cent of those of our subjects who had only experienced one OBE in their life considered, when responding to a questionnaire, that their time sense had been distorted in connection with their OBE. This figure rose to 37 per cent among those who had had more than one experience and may therefore be considered to have had a greater opportunity to notice any such effect (Green, 1968b).

It is worth noting that according to Oswald (1962) it is quite possible for short episodes of sleep lasting a few seconds to occur while the subject's eyes remain open throughout. Oswald adduces evidence from both his own and other people's laboratories for this phenomenon. In the case of his own experiments, subjects who were exposed to repeated electric shocks, timed to synchronise with loud jazz music and with powerful lights which flashed on and off in front of the subjects' faces, showed the electrophysiological signs of sleep even when their eyes were 'glued and strapped so widely open that the pupil remained exposed wherever the eye was turned'. More protracted episodes of sleep with the eyes open can apparently be observed in children, and adults suffering from dehydration.

If the present hypothesis is correct, it might provide a framework in which one could account for the fact that paralysis is reported in connection with some OBEs but not others. It may be that the minority of cases in which paralysis is reported occur in a form of sleep similar if not identical to REM sleep, with its cortical excitement and motor inhibition. The remainder, and in particular those in which the subject continues with some motor activity, might occur in Stage 1 sleep, or something very like it. Stage 1 is the first phase of sleep into which one enters when leaving the waking state, whereas REM sleep usually only occurs after one has passed through both Stage 1 and SWS stages. There are two differences between Stage 1 and REM sleep which are important for our present discussion. First, rapid eye movements are usually absent in Stage 1; and secondly, Stage 1, like SWS, is not characterised by the extreme motor inhibition of REM sleep. In other respects REM and Stage 1 sleep are considered by some writers to be similar to each other. REM sleep is indeed sometimes referred to as 'ascending' or 'emergent' Stage 1 sleep to convey the fact that electrophysiologically it shows a considerable resemblance to 'descending' Stage 1 (that occurring prior to the subject descending into deeper, slow-wave stages).

The present hypothesis would also seem to fit with the phenomenological relationship between lucid dreams and out-of-the body experiences. As we discussed in Chapter 7, the two classes of experience seem to be for the most part phenomenologically distinct, but there are ambiguous cases which are difficult to classify unequivocally one way rather than the other – the situation represented in Figure 6.1 (p. 55) by two distinct but partially overlapping ellipses. These phenomenological data would appear to fit well with the hypothesis that most but not all OBEs occur in conjunction with a form of Stage 1 sleep, while most but not all lucid dreams occur in association with REM sleep.

One argument which has been used in the past, for example by Blackmore (1983), to reject the idea that OBEs are associated with sleep, is that they are phenomenologically quite distinct from ordinary dreams. The subject of an OBE will quite commonly assert that 'it was nothing like a dream'. However, lucid dreams and false awakenings can be 'nothing like a dream' in the same sense; and we have seen that lucid dreams have been found to be most usually associated electrophysiologically with REM sleep, while we have suggested above that there is indirect evidence for false awakenings being likewise associated with REM. If lucid dreams and false awakenings, which are quite different phenomenologically from ordinary dreams, can nevertheless be associated with electrophysiological sleep, then we see no a priori reason why OBEs should not be so associated also.

PARALYSIS AND APPARITIONAL EXPERIENCES

Paralysis was claimed by a small proportion (fewer than 3 per cent) of the subjects reporting apparitional experiences to Green and McCreery (1975). In view of the present proposal that the various metachoric experiences should be regarded as forming a continuum, rather than a set of discrete and unrelated phenomena, it is interesting to note that out-of-the-body and apparitional experiences may occur in close temporal association with one another. By way of introduction to the question of paralysis in relation to apparitional hallucinations, we will quote a case in which an ecsomatic experience was immediately preceded by an auditory hallucination. The paralysis seems to have preceded both the auditory and the ecsomatic parts of the hallucinatory experience.

The second occurrence was at home. I was tired and went to bed late after my mother, my father being out on call. About half an hour after I was in bed, I found myself unable to move my legs, arms or shut my eyes (I was lying on my back). I started sweating and got very frightened. A little while later I heard a voice, like that of an old man reciting verses as in the Bible. I cannot remember what he said. I thought this noise was coming from a cupboard in my room and I thought I would investigate, but I could not move anything. Within a very short time I had a strange feeling of leaving my feet, legs, body, etc., and being completely in my head. I could not feel my body. Then I literally squeezed upwards and found myself floating away with a light (blue white) joining me to my body which I could see lying on the bed. As soon as I realised my body was 'over there' I heard a door slam, just like our front door, and found myself in my bed shivering and lying in a pool of cold sweat, absolutely terrified. I got up and dashed downstairs thinking my father had returned. There was no one there and the front door was open. I had seen my mother shut it and check it before she went to bed, it was definitely shut properly then. I then went upstairs and looked in my mother's room, she was there sleeping.

Another point that may be of relevance to the hypothesis of continuity between the various metachoric experiences is that about a quarter of all the apparitional cases reported to us occurred just after waking, usually during the night. We think it is possible that at least some of these were unidentified false awakenings. Subjects who experience Type 2 false awakenings sometimes do not identify them as hallucinatory until they have experienced several of them and have been able to work out by experimental tests, completed in the waking state, that the events they seem to experience do not really happen.

It would be possible to argue that the experience just quoted may have been such an unidentified false awakening and that an observer would have seen the subject lying asleep throughout the experience. If this interpretation is correct the paralysis might well be regarded as a sign that the subject was in a state at least resembling REM sleep.

This hypothesis may even be maintained in a case such as the following in which the subject at first seems to have been able to move normally while hallucinating an apparition but then at a later stage in the experience felt herself paralysed.

> My experience took place in a bright sunny bedroom in (New York's) 90 degree heat. . . .
> I had just completed a sixteen hour shift, on-duty in a maternity unit. On returning to my apartment building, I was met by the superintendent who warned me that my apartment was to be included in a plumbing inspector's visit that a.m.
> Utterly exhausted and desperate for sleep as I was due back on-duty at the hospital at 3:30 p.m . . . . I collapsed into bed. I willed myself to sleep and believe I dozed off. I woke, aware of a presence. On looking up, I saw a man bending over the bed.
> I instinctively, ostrich like, closed my eyes and tugged the sheet over me. Inwardly furious at the man's impertinence (I assumed him to be the plumbing inspector) I thought him extremely objectionable as all the apartments were similar and he couldn't mistake the bedroom for the bathroom.
> Then, reason asserted itself. I kept the chain on the door and previously when someone had unlocked it, the crash of the chain had wakened me. I could never sleep through that. . . .
> I recalled the man's appearance so vividly. He had snowy white hair, ruddy cheeks and wore a rough Harris tweed jacket. I didn't recognise him as I'd closed my eyes so quickly. I reasoned that I must have had a hallucination and tried to open my eyes. I soon discovered that I was unable to do so and my limbs and body felt leaden and I couldn't move. This unfamiliar sensation suddenly lifted. No one was there. I rose and checked that the chain was still in place.
>
> (Green and McCreery, 1975, pp. 128–9)

In this case we would argue that the entire experience may have been a false awakening up to the point at which the subject experienced the paralysis; in other words, the subject's supposed movements in pulling the sheet over herself may have been hallucinatory, just like the visual part of the experience – the seeing of the man in the Harris tweed jacket. On this interpretation an observer would have seen the subject lying apparently asleep until the moment when the paralysis lifted. The apparent 'onset' of the paralysis simply represented the point at which the subject ceased to hallucinate movements and found herself temporarily unable to make real ones.

To what extent could the sleep hypothesis be extended to cover all apparitional experiences? At first sight it is even harder than in the case of OBEs to imagine that all apparition cases occur during episodes of sleep, since the subjects of apparitional experiences seem more often to be active at the time of the experience than the subjects of OBEs. As mentioned above, three-quarters of those reporting only one OBE to us were lying down at the time of the experience, whereas the comparable figure in the case of our apparition subjects was 38 per cent. However, only 20 per cent of the apparition subjects considered they were actually moving about at the time of their experience, as opposed to lying, sitting or standing still. Moreover, we must consider the possibility that some of the movements in this 20 per cent of cases may themselves have been hallucinatory. For example, in one case reported to us the subject describes playing with an apparitional dog in a garden at night over a period which seems to have lasted a matter of minutes (see Green and McCreery, 1975, pp. 144-5). In a case such as this it is possible, on the metachoric interpretation, that an independent observer would simply have seen the subject standing with an abstracted air for the duration of the experience, and not moving at all.

There are certain cases in which it is clear that the movements which the visually hallucinated subject thought himself to be making during the experience did not match the movements he actually made. In one such case the subject was under the impression that a figure of a man, which subsequently turned out to be hallucinatory, had lifted a veranda blind for him to assist his passage into a house from the garden. However, an independent observer sitting on the veranda at the time attested that the subject had lifted the blind for himself (see Green and McCreery, 1975, pp. 33-4, for a full account of this case). Reports of such cases, in which there is a clear-cut conflict between the experience of the percipient and independent evidence such as the testimony of a non-hallucinated bystander, are relatively hard to find. But this may be at least in part because suitable circumstances seldom arise for such discrepancies to occur and be noticed. Many apparitional experiences happen when the subject is alone, and when there is a non-hallucinated bystander this second person is unlikely to be preoccupied, either at the time or afterwards, with the theoretical question of whether or to what extent the percipient was hallucinating his or her own movements, if any, in addition to whatever visual hallucination was being experienced.[1]

Another obstacle to an interpretation of all apparitional experiences in terms of a sleep mechanism might seem to be the fact that the subjects are usually not aware of any discontinuity of consciousness at the start or end of their experience. When questioned on this point 92 per cent of our subjects said that they had noticed no such discontinuity.

However, it may be relevant in this context to draw attention to the phenomenon of what Oswald (1962) calls the 'micro-sleep'. This refers to the fact that someone may fall asleep for short periods without subsequent awareness of having done so. Moreover, the subject may strongly deny having slept, although the EEG record shows unambiguous sleep patterns. For example, Oswald reproduces part of the EEG record of a man

> who was supposed to move ceaselessly in rhythmic fashion to synchronized flashing lights and rhythmic music while his eyes were glued widely open. He was not sleep-deprived, yet in a 25-minute period he ceased moving 52 times, each such occasion being accompanied by EEG signs of sleep and slowing of the heart. Questioned afterwards, he was adamant that he had stopped moving only once. He recalled having been aware, early in the 25-minute period, of luminous geometrical patterns but could recall nothing of further mental experiences.
>
> (Oswald, 1962, p. 65)

A possible objection to this analogy between apparitional experiences and micro-sleeps might be that by definition the apparitional subject is not amnesic for the content of his or her putative sleep episode, as Oswald's subject was for most of his, otherwise the apparition subject would not be reporting his or her experience after the event. However, there are a number of differences between the two situations. First, the sleep episodes of Oswald's subject were experimentally induced, whereas the putative sleep episodes corresponding to apparitional experiences appear to be completely spontaneous. Secondly, there may be a difference in time-scale in the two situations, apparitional experiences apparently lasting longer, typically, than the type of micro-sleep studied by Oswald in the laboratory.

The idea that hallucinations may represent the intrusion into waking consciousness of processes normally associated with sleep has been proposed before, for example by Feinberg (1970), who specifically confines the idea to the visual hallucinations of drug-withdrawal delirium. However, the hypothesis seems to have made relatively little headway as a general theory of hallucinations. Part of the reason may be that the model has proposed a link between hallucinations and REM sleep, rather than with any other phase. Thus Feinberg specifically suggests that drug-withdrawal hallucinations represent 'the intrusion of high levels of REM into waking'. Studies of actively hallucinating schizophrenic patients, however, did not find the features, such as rapid eye movements, specific to REM sleep. As Robbins (1988) puts it, 'The physiological correlates of dreaming and hallucinations appear to be different.'

There are two points of relevance here. First, dreams, even of the dramatic, narrative type to which the term 'dream' is usually restricted, do not occur exclusively in association with REM sleep. The association is not as one-to-one as was believed when rapid eye movements were first observed in the 1950s. So there is no reason why we should confine our search for electrophysiological evidence of sleep in connection with hallucinations to the characteristics of REM sleep in particular. Secondly, there is in any case no need to identify hallucinations exclusively with dreams of the dramatic, narrative type, since there can clearly be phenomenological differences between the two types of experience. It might be argued that, for example, apparitional experiences in normal subjects show a greater phenomenological resemblance to the sorts of experience, such as hypnagogic imagery, which are already known to be associated with Stage 1 sleep.

Incidentally, it would seem more logical a priori to look for parallels, if not identity, between the neurophysiology of hallucinations and descending Stage 1 sleep rather than REM, since by definition waking hallucinations begin from the waking state, as does Stage 1 sleep, whereas REM phases normally arise from non-REM phases of sleep rather than from waking consciousness.

CONCLUSION

In conclusion, we suggest that the occasional appearance of paralysis in the various different hallucinatory states under consideration – lucid dreaming, false awakenings, ecsomatic experiences, and apparitions – supports the view that there is a degree of continuity between them. We further propose that the factor making for this continuity may be sleep in its various manifestations or phases.

In addition, we suggest that a characteristic that many examples of totally hallucinatory experience have in common is a 'paradoxical' combination of muscular relaxation with cortical arousal. We will be considering the significance of this combination for the question of what individual differences may predispose a person to experience any or all of these states in Chapter 15.

Chapter 9

Control of lucid dreams

Lucidity is sometimes defined as the awareness, on the part of the dreamer, that he is the 'author' of his own dream. There is a corresponding tendency on the part of some writers to emphasise the potential which the lucid dreamer has to control the content of his or her experience, indeed even to assume that a lucid dreamer has unlimited control over what he or she dreams. These ideas, however, are rather misleading. The lucid dreamer may recognise the status of what he is experiencing as 'unreal', but if he regards it as something of which his own mind is the author, this is by way of a theoretical speculation, and involves him in a belief in a subconscious mind which operates independently of his conscious volition.

In fact, apart from movements and relocations of his dream body analogous to those available to him in waking life, a lucid dreamer may appear to have little, if any, control over the development of events within his dream. Lucidity may appear to provide him with little more than the position of a passive spectator of events, albeit one more emotionally detached than before he realised the true status of his experience.

Lucid dreamers may successfully remember that they wish to carry out certain intentions, but as the following dream shows, their control of the situation is by no means complete and they may have to await with patient curiosity the means by which their dream will fulfil their wishes, if at all. The narrator in this account is Embury Brown.

'What will I see out of the window?' I wonder, vaguely aware that I am dreaming, and fearing that it may wake me to look out .... I jump up into the air to make sure that I am dreaming

(my standard test lately, and an infallible one) . . . . The first
jump is light and feathery, but I do not go very high . . . . I am
now fully aware that it must be a dream. 'This is a lucid
dream', I announce to my brother with great elation, thinking:
'How strange and gratifying that another dream has come so
soon.' (No. 78 was just two days before.) My brother, however,
has disappeared: well, I can manage my dream alone. I consider what to do. I remember that I have planned to 'call' (as Dr
van Eeden 'called' images of deceased friends) a taxi, and to
have a lucid dream to be named 'Going Places'. 'Taxi!' I shout,
'taxi!' I meet a hotel employee and ask, 'Where do I get a taxi?'
'Downstairs at the desk,' he says, and thither I immediately
descend by a short stairway. 'Taxi?' I say to a uniformed young
man who rises and leads me out to where a sport roadster is
parked . . . . He starts the car and turns onto a broad suburban
avenue which I at first turn take to be 'Twelfth Avenue by the
Hudson River'. I consider asking to be taken to some theatre,
but do not remember the name of any. It occurs to me that I
need not talk to the driver, as he is not a real separate
personality. 'I suppose you know where I am to go,' I say, and
he nods affirmatively. It is more than *I* know, and I hope he
will not take me to some undesirable dive. I bring a handful of
coins out of my pocket, hoping that my dream-money will
appear in convenient denominations. I turn my thoughts to the
earlier stages of the dream to fix them in my mind; but it is a
fatal mistake. Attempting to return to the taxi-scene, I find it
wholly vanished. I can reconstruct it imaginatively, but in such
day-dreaming I do not get anywhere. It does not take hold, and
so I resign myself to waking up. But I was far from being
awake: what followed was but a false awakening, in which I
gather up my handful of coins from among the bedclothes in a
baseball grandstand. Then I really wake up.

(Brown, 1936, p. 62)

Attempts to affect the environment by dream volition in a way
which would be described as supernatural or miraculous if it
occurred in waking life seem always to be somewhat uncertain in
their effect. The result that a dreamer wants to produce is often
delayed, and when it occurs it may or may not conform to his
original intentions. The following two examples from one of our
own subjects illustrate this process.

Again a busy environment – like a fair. I become lucid. Realise it's a dream and I have control. See a large, old-fashioned looking car/van. Point at it and command it to disappear. After a couple of goes it starts to fade away.

I see some sort of tall crane device. Have a go at ordering it to disappear. Parts of its structure fade until only a little tall, spindly crane-like thing remains.

(Subject N.C.)

On the whole, then, a lucid dreamer is presented with dream events in much the same way as an ordinary dreamer, and the control which he is able to exercise is limited and uncertain in its effects. Thus, for example, he may be presented with a landscape and may deliberately choose what route to follow within it, or he may find himself in a certain situation and think of experiments which, in these circumstances, he would like to carry out. But choice of scene or location within a lucid dream is not altogether easy to effect; subjects may imagine how they would like the scene to change, but the way in which it does so, and the extent to which it fulfils their wishes, may take them by surprise.

Nevertheless, some dreamers have learnt specific methods which they have found assist them in exercising some degree of control over the scenery and course of events within the dream, and we will now discuss some of these.

Several subjects have found that covering or closing their eyes in the lucid dream, and thinking of the change of scene which they would like to see on reopening them, has had the effect of producing the desired scene, or at least something approximating to it.

The eye-covering technique has also, incidentally, been found by some lucid dreamers to be a method of awakening oneself. One lucid dreamer who uses it in this way, Subject E, also suggests withdrawing one's attention from the sequence of dream events at the same time as cutting them off visually by covering the eyes.

The first development beyond lucid dreaming was the discovery of how to wake myself out of a dream. The method, which I discovered quite by chance in an ordinary dream while hiding from pursuers, consists in covering my eyes with my hands and withdrawing my thoughts from the dream. There would follow a prolonged and most unpleasant sensation as though trying to get back into my body which I could sense but not move. Thereafter in unpleasant dreams I tended to remember this method of escape, and I also experimented with it in lucid dreams. With repetition the transition became quite easy, although sometimes instead of waking up I would find myself in a different dream, not necessarily lucid.

(Subject E)

Another method which, it is claimed, has been found to be effective in producing awakening, is focusing on some point of the visual environment within the dream, whether a stationary or a moving one. Paul Tholey appears to regard this as a reliable method (Tholey and Utecht, 1987). However, the reports which the present writers have received suggest that any procedure for awakening oneself from a lucid dream is liable to be an unreliable one, which may on occasion be followed by a normal dream or some form of false awakening rather than by genuine awakening.

Stephen LaBerge advocates the curious technique of spinning like a top in order to prolong or stabilise lucidity in the dream state. He suggests pirouetting, while in a standing position in the dream, ideally with the arms outstretched like a whirling dervish. Whatever the particular variant of the technique being adopted, the objective is apparently to generate a strong feeling of movement in the dream. LaBerge also recommends that one should strongly remind oneself while spinning that one is dreaming and that one wants to go on being aware of the fact while performing the actions (cf. LaBerge, 1985). He claims that the method, which he initially evolved from his own experience of lucid dreaming, has also been found by a number of his subjects to facilitate a change of scene in accordance with their wishes. LaBerge himself usually found that the dream scene which appeared when he stopped spinning consisted of his own bedroom. Indeed, on the first occasion he experimented with the technique, he thought, erroneously, that he had woken up. But he believes this may be an accidental result of the circumstances in which he discovered the technique. Even if this were not the case, a false awakening could, he believes, be avoided by reminding oneself during the spinning transition that one is dreaming.

LaBerge speculates that the method may work by stimulating the vestibular system of the brain (the part that might be involved in generating the images of spinning), which in turn may help to activate nearby brain areas involved in the generation of the rapid eye movements characteristic of lucidly dreaming sleep. Ingenious though this hypothesis appears at first sight, we wonder whether alternative explanations may not eventually be found, if the effect proves to be a reliable one. It seem to us that the rapid eye movements of REM sleep are more likely the relatively peripheral effect, rather than the central cause, of the cortically activated state which REM sleep represents. It would be odd, therefore, if amplifying or prolonging this peripheral effect were to amplify or prolong the central cause. It seems to us that the effect of spinning in the dream might simply be to increase arousal directly, perhaps because of the bizarre or unaccustomed nature of the dream 'action'.

It is interesting to compare the subject's degree of control in lucid dreams with attempts to regulate the content of hypnagogic imagery. Leaning (1925) comments on the 'wilfulness' of the latter, and found that many of the published and unpublished accounts she reviewed reported no control at all over the occurrence, content or development of the images. However, some subjects had developed an indirect method of influencing the content by thinking of what they wanted to see and waiting for apparently spontaneous changes to occur. For example, one subject wrote: 'I say to myself curiously "That resembles a frog (an alligator, or what not)." Forthwith, the image transforms itself into a frog.' Another subject's imagery took the form of a continuous panoramic landscape, and Leaning writes: 'this could be modified, as from flat country to hilly, or adorned with the blossoms of springtide fruit-trees, but the changes were a natural development of what was already in process.' Apparently, if this subject 'willed' an unlikely thing, it 'did not come'.

One common limitation on control of the perceptual environment reported by lucid dreamers consists in being unable to control the general level of illumination. In particular, a number of Keith Hearne's subjects have reported that they were unable to make the level of illumination alter appropriately when they tried turning a light switch on or off in their dreams. This is a topic we will discuss in more detail in Chapter 10.

THE EROTIC ELEMENT IN LUCID DREAMS

Attempts to introduce erotic elements into lucid dreams seem to be variable in their results, depending very much, it would appear, on the individual dreamer concerned. At the time of writing *Lucid Dreams*, the case material suggested that most subjects found it difficult to engage in sexual activity, or even to have mildly erotic encounters, without loss of lucidity, a fact which they tended to ascribe to its interfering with the emotional detachment which they regarded as necessary for the maintenance of insight. Subject E, for example, claims that there is an inhibition against it, and Oliver Fox appears to have found it ruled out by the necessity for complete emotional detachment. Other lucid dreamers, such as Subject A, have found it possible to engage in amorous activities but have found it impossible not to awake before the culmination of the experience. Other subjects again, such as Subject C, comment on the difficulty of retaining lucidity when entering into any activity of this kind.

The Marquis d'Hervey de Saint-Denys appears at one time to have gone to some considerable trouble to ensure the appearance of two desired ladies of his acquaintance in his dreams. For example, at the dances he went to he took care to waltz with each lady when a certain specific tune was being played, and provided himself with a musical box capable of playing the relevant tunes while he was asleep. The procedure apparently succeeded in evoking in his dreams the figure of the lady associated with the tune which he had set his musical box to play. The Marquis is not very informative about how the situation developed once he had secured the appearance of the selected lady companion, or whether the dreams were lucid at any stage, but he appears in general to have had a high opinion of lucid dreams as a means of experiencing whatever the heart could desire (Hervey de Saint-Denys, 1867).

Even at the time of writing *Lucid Dreams* we knew of at least one subject, an elderly gentleman, who claimed to have used lucid dreams to supplement his otherwise meagre love life. The subject, now deceased, did not wish to be identified but gave the following account of his experiences. The account is written in the third person as having happened to a friend of his, but verbally he acknowledged that the experiences were his own and actually made a significant contribution to his life, which was otherwise rather dull in these respects.

A *friend* of mine who realised his ability to interfere in his dreams got into the habit of approaching good-looking girls in his dreams and disrobing them. He reasoned that as they were merely the products of his own mind no harm could be done. If this is not so nice blame *him*, not me!

Anyway on the first occasion he dreamed of a girl whom he knew and proceeded to undress her. Another girl, very beautiful, came along, voluntarily stripped and lay down. As the papers put it intercourse took place and he woke up with an orgasm.

According to him, and knowing him *well* I believe him, the tactile, thermal, etc., sensations were just as real, in the sense of a complete duplication, as the waking experience would be.

As far as I can remember *he* had a few of these dreams and then the Superego seemed to intervene and no more ladies enlivened his nights when he was aware that he was dreaming. Alas!

Some more recent lucid dreamers, notably Patricia Garfield, have not only considered sex possible in lucid dreams, but have spoken in glowing terms of its intensely ecstatic nature (Garfield, 1974).

Stephen LaBerge has carried out laboratory experiments aimed at studying the physiological accompaniments of sex in lucid dreams, with results which will be discussed in Chapter 13, on possible therapeutic applications of lucid dreaming. The fact that he has found such experiments practicable at all argues that at least some of his subjects, predominantly female ones, are able to dream lucidly of sexual activity without loss of insight.

INHIBITIONS IN LUCID DREAMS

One respect in which the dreamer's control may not be complete in a lucid dream is that he may find it difficult to overcome his inhibitions about carrying out actions which would be physically dangerous either to himself or to others if he were to perform them in real life, despite being aware of the unreality of dream events. In this respect it may be relevant to compare the lucid dreamer with someone under hypnosis who, although he appears to some extent under the control of the hypnotist, is none the less supposed to be incapable of performing actions which he would not be willing to perform in the normal state.

A behaviour which several lucid dreamers have attempted is that of 'committing suicide' in a lucid dream. At least two people experienced considerable difficulty in accomplishing this task. The Marquis d'Hervey de Saint-Denys once tried to cut his throat with a razor in a lucid dream, but writes: 'My instinctive horror of the action I wished to simulate proved stronger than my conscious volition' (d'Hervey de Saint-Denys, 1867; quoted in McCreery, 1973). On other occasions he considered trying to shoot himself in a lucid dream but reports that obtaining and operating a pistol always took so long that his attention was deflected from the purpose in hand. More recently, a subject has described trying to commit suicide in a car while dreaming lucidly:

> This morning, I had awakened from 5:00-6:30 a.m to actually drive toward the beach to view a comet visible in the eastern, dawning sky. It was quite cold out, so I had worn gloves while driving the VW bus. I had returned home and went back to sleep by 6:30 a.m.
> One of the ensuing dreams was of driving in the van. I looked at my right hand, gloved, and brought upon the conscious/unconscious state. . . . I suddenly recalled my experiment objective of dream-suicide, and saw the perfect opportunity. However, I first 'checked' with myself to make certain I was dreaming . . . , and then purposely, consciously veered off the road toward some trees. The van came to an abrupt halt before touching the trees, however, not as part of my conscious directive, but of the subconscious, as if strong brakes had been applied. The scene then faded and blurred.
> (Marcot, 1987, p. 69)

A possible counter-example, in which someone did succeed in simulating suicide in a lucid dream, was provided by one of the Institute's consultants, the late Colin Cherry, Professor of Electrical Engineering at Imperial College, London, who had occasional lucid dreams and wrote us the following account of one of them.

> I was walking about a large meadow which sloped down towards a main road on which there was traffic. I was saying to myself that 'I am dreaming so let's test this out by jumping under one of those cars.' I ran down the hill and jumped under a car, then I woke. I could not repeat that dream.

Another of our subjects, Subject E, experienced great difficulty in accomplishing a less extreme form of self-damage than suicide, namely trying to pierce her hand with a skewer in a lucid dream. She reports that initially the skewer would not penetrate her hand despite repeated attempts. Finally she succeeded, but experienced no pain as a result (see McCreery, 1973, pp. 111–12).

A similar inhibition may operate with regard to attempts to physically injure, and especially kill, another person in one's lucid dream. Embury Brown provided the following detailed description of his attempt to hang someone while lucid. It is interesting to note that although he eventually succeeded in performing the requisite actions, despite the strong inhibition he experienced, the 'victim' of his experiment did not 'die' as he expected.

May 7, 1934. (An eleven o'clock supper of mince pies and milk may explain the unpleasantness but not the lucidity of the following. I arose at 6 a.m. remembering to put out a milk bottle, being alone in the house, and then went back to bed.) I see a boy in the kitchen, then a man. How did they get in with all the doors locked? Then with some elation I discern: 'It's a dream; now I can experiment.' I remember that I have thought, among other things, of trying murder in a lucid dream, and so I attempt to tear the boy limb from limb, but I cannot make the least impression on his body with my hands. The experiment is distasteful and I desist. I pass into an unfamiliar room, a kind of woodshed with a pit seven feet deep in the center. A man sits on the steps that lead into the pit. At first he is our friend the Rev. Mr. ——, but later he is more like a young hobo. I tell him he must be hanged. There is a noose dangling on the opposite side of the pit, and an apparatus for winding it up. I find myself precariously poised aloft, trying to adjust the rope. I draw down what I adjudge to be a sufficient length and then descend to the rim of the pit. 'You are about to enter the next world', I tell the young man. Again I feel an aversion to continuing the experiment, but reflect that it is certainly a dream, and can do no real harm, while it may be both interesting and informative if carried out. 'Perhaps,' I think, 'if I somewhat let go of the reality of the situation, it will seem more tolerable.' *I withdraw all imaginative cooperation from the dreaming function*, at the seeming risk of waking, but am satisfied to observe that I do not wake up, though the objects in the room have a very reassuring dream-like vagueness. 'It is certainly possible – indeed now actual – to conduct introspections in a dream,' I notice. The young man has obediently come round to be hanged. He jumps onto a chair that stands on the floor of the pit. 'He thinks he is to be lifted from there,' I reflect; 'evidently he does not understand hanging.' I tell him to come back up. I adjust the noose, and, again reassuring myself with the thought that I am obviously acting in a mere dream-world, I lift the boy and plunge him into the pit. I almost expect the shock to tear the head from his body, but it does not even kill him. On the floor of the pit he sits up and raises his hands to his neck, seeming to suffer a great pain. As I stand looking down at him, I wake up.

(Brown, 1936, pp. 64–5)

A somewhat contrasting example, in which a lucid dreamer knocked out the front teeth of someone in her dream without any apparent inhibition, is quoted in Chapter 13 (pp. 133–4).

On the whole, it is the impression of the authors that control of lucid dreams depends to a large extent on working within a pattern of existing psychological associations and anticipations. This pattern does not, however, necessarily correspond completely to the realities of waking life. Certain departures of a surreal kind seem to be relatively 'acceptable', and these departures show some correspondence with certain 'magical' traditions. Thus, flying and the movement or transmutation of fairly small objects seem to be easily accessible, as they are in fairy stories and in fantasy films of the *Superman* variety.

On the other hand, some common elements in fantasy stories, such as the sudden shrinking of a human being or his transmutation into some other creature, such as a dog or a toad, do not seem to feature in lucid dreams, at least not frequently. On the whole, it seems to be the more positive features of magical tradition which are made use of by lucid dreamers. To be able to fly, and to exercise some degree of magical control over the environment, are positive experiences, whereas to be transmuted oneself in some diminishing way, or to diminish some other person, are not completely unambiguous forms of satisfaction.

It might be thought that exercising one's powers to bring about unpleasant effects on other people might in certain circumstances give some sense of gratification, but attempts to do destructive things to other people in lucid dreams seem to be somewhat inhibited and appear to be limited to simple physical operations such as hitting them with more or less the same force as would be used in waking life.

CONCLUSION

We might conclude therefore, at least tentatively, that any relaxation of moral restraints within lucid dreams is restricted to some extent by the strength of expectations derived from waking experience, and in particular by the reluctance which one normally experiences to risk damaging oneself or other people. The latter resistance would appear to have a good deal of force, if one considers that lucid dreamers would appear theoretically to have the potential for reproducing for their own amusement, without any of the usual risks, the occurrences of the less attractive kind of horror film as well as those of the more pleasant fantasies.

Similar considerations concerning the carry-over effect of waking expectations may help account for the sorts of 'miracle' which are and are not common features of lucid dreams. Thus it may be that, for some reason, people have never acquired a very strong impression of the difficulty of flying, even though they have done no more than jump in normal life. But they have learned that walls resist attempts to push through them; and perhaps this is why passing through walls in lucid dreams, although sometimes possible, is usually attended by distinctive and unusual sensations. (See, for example, McCreery, 1973, pp. 116–17.)

Chapter 10

Two areas of difficulty
Reading and switching on lights

We have already drawn attention to the relatively high degree of realism that can be achieved by lucid dreams when compared with non-lucid ones, particularly with respect to the question of perceptual quality. However, in this chapter we will focus on two types of dream event which seem to highlight with relative consistency certain limitations of the dream process. These two types of event are reading and the switching on (or off) of lights. It is worth devoting particular attention to such frequently reported breakdowns in the realism of the lucid dream experience as their study may contribute to our understanding of the nature of the lucid dream and its relation to other quasi-perceptual experiences, as well as possibly pointing to underlying brain processes involved in 'generating' these quasi-perceptual experiences.

READING IN LUCID DREAMS

The following example of Moers-Messmer illustrates the sort of difficulties which can be encountered when trying to read textual material in a lucid dream. Like another of Moers-Messmer's cases quoted in Chapter 4 (p. 26), it shows the dreamer having some initial success in reading, but then finding the task becoming too difficult for him. Finally he is able to 'read' again, but this time the symbols are hieroglyphic-like. Presumably these symbols did not correspond to anything Moers-Messmer knew in reality. Interestingly, however, he seems in the dream to 'know' what the symbols mean.

> I realise that I am dreaming for a reason which I have forgotten. I find myself in my usual room. The sun is shining

outside. I look at it. . . . Afterwards on looking inside the room
I have bright spots for several seconds. As soon as they have
vanished, I pick up a newspaper which is lying on the table
and read without difficulty. Then I attempt to read the
individual words backwards. As I do so there are many more
letters than belong to the corresponding words. When I have
read several words in this way, partly forwards and partly
backwards, something remarkable happens. Some of them
have changed their shape; they no longer consist of the usual
letters, but form figures which bear a distinct resemblance to
hieroglyphics. And now I can see nothing but these symbols,
each of which signifies a word or syllable, the ordinary letters
having completely disappeared. I know exactly what each
symbol signifies, and run my eyes over them in the usual
direction from left to right and read entire sentences without
any effort.

(Moers-Messmer, 1938, Case 10)

In the following example, Embury Brown describes an
apparently successful experiment in reading, but the task he set
himself seems to have been a fairly simple one.

At a desk by a window I think: 'I am asleep'. I hold up my
hand. 'If I wake myself now, will I find that I am sitting at the
desk with my hand really in some other position?' I prefer to
go on dreaming. 'I am near waking, here at this desk,' I think,
'but if I am careful I may avoid full awakening.' I look out of
the window and picture myself standing outside on the
veranda-roof; *but this piece of dream-daydreaming does not become
a dream reality. I am still at the desk.* I have a book with an index.
'I have never in a dream looked up anything with an index. I
will try it.' Quite realistically I verify an indexed title. I walk
about the room. . . . I continue the dream but without lucidity,
waking at 7:00 a.m., surprised that I was really sleeping not in
a desk chair but in bed.

(Brown, 1936, p. 64)

Our Subject E has the following general comments to make about
her attempts to read in lucid dreams.

Curiously, reading in lucid dreams, and remembering the
words, seems more difficult than in ordinary dreams – perhaps
this is because one tends to look in these circumstances for

something specially significant. Occasionally there takes place a phenomenon which might be described as automatic writing, speaking or singing, in which I am aware of the words (or notes) as they come but not in advance, and simultaneously I am very much aware of, and intrigued by, the situation. Although the words appear meaningful at the time they are extremely difficult to retain in the memory, and I manage to bring back only an occasional phrase: e.g. 'breezes softly sing and sway'.

Another person who seems to have experienced difficulties in reading in his lucid dreams is Oliver Fox (see Green, 1968a, p. 72). At the same time it should be mentioned that Green found one case in which a subject read an apparently convincing text ('a kind of proclamation or set of instructions') during which process 'two or three lines of writing were clearly in focus at any one time' (Green, 1968, p. 72).

One possible explanation for the difficulties which can be experienced with reading in lucid dreams is that they are related to the need that the subject may feel not to take the dream too seriously on its own terms in order to maintain insight into the situation. After all, one implication of the realisation that one is dreaming ought to be that no printed matter which appears can be anything other than the product of one's own mind (unless the possibility of ESP is invoked). So in a sense the dreamer 'ought' only to view written matter with, at most, disinterested curiosity, in the spirit of 'I wonder what my subconscious has come up with here!'. Any other attitude might lead to a sort of immersion in the reality of the dream which would be incompatible with insight. It may be relevant to reflect on how immersed one can become during waking life when reading. One may indeed become quite oblivious to one's perceptual surroundings, and absorbed in the themes or concepts evoked by the printed word. If a corresponding process of absorption were to occur in a lucid dream it might completely dispel the original 'perceptual' environment (as in the case of Embury Brown's dream quoted on pp. 95–6) and the insight that went with the perception of the original scene.

On a more biological level, it is possible that reading difficulties in lucid dreams are an indication of relative depression of function in the left hemisphere of the brain. In Chapter 15 we will be putting forward the hypothesis that a left hemisphere relatively inactive in comparison with the right may be a general characteristic of the lucid dreaming state. If this is correct it might help to explain the difficulty that tends to be experienced with written material. The left hemisphere is thought to be preferentially involved in the processing of information in a sequential as opposed to a global, holistic fashion (see Table 15.1 on p. 158), and reading letters and words would seem to be an example of such serial processing.

It is interesting to note that reading difficulties have been observed in the case of other forms of 'involuntary' imagery. For example, Saltmarsh (1925), having described how in the hypnagogic state, in addition to visual phenomena, he is liable to have sentences or phrases enter his mind in an involuntary way, adds: '[The sentence or phrase] is usually completely non-sensical'. This type of hypnagogic experience usually occurred without any pseudo-auditory or other sensory accompaniment, but on occasion Saltmarsh experienced it 'mixed up with the visual type'. He writes: 'In these instances I have a hypnagogic vision of a printed book which I try to read. I never succeed in getting more than about half a line, and it is always the same sort of nonsense.'

Ardis and McKellar (1956), after quoting this example of Saltmarsh's, comment: 'We have observed similar imagery of "jumbled print" under mescaline and, as possibly a related phenomenon, images of numbers appearing upside down.'

An interesting point is that to Oliver Fox the print he would see in his lucid dreams 'seems clear enough until one tries to read it'. In other words, there seems to be a discrepancy between the appearance or face-value of the image and its true informational content.

Overall, the point which seems to emerge is that quasi-perceptual imagery and hallucinations of all kinds are not necessarily to be taken at face value as regards their apparent informational content. That is to say, while having the appear-ance to the subject of being highly detailed, this appearance may in fact break down under close attentional scrutiny and be revealed as merely an appearance, or indeed as an illusion.

Accepting this reservation, however, should not necessarily be taken as downgrading quasi-perceptual experiences relative to actual perception. The latter may itself contain a large element of 'bluff'. It has long been noted that objectively only the central part of the field of vision can be clearly defined at a given time, since the physiology of the retina is such that the ability to resolve detail falls away as the distance from the central area, the fovea, increases. Yet we do not characteristically have the experience of seeing the world as blurred except for a 'tunnel' of clear vision straight ahead of us. Similarly, it can easily be demonstrated that we have an objective 'blind spot' as a result of the passage of the optic nerve through the retina, yet this spot appears to be 'filled in' experientially so that we are never troubled by it. (This fact may be contrasted with the effects of damage to the visual system which can result, at least initially, in persistent *scotomata*, or areas of subjectively experienced blindness, within the field of vision.)

SWITCHING ON LIGHTS

Several reports have described the difficulty of switching on an electric light in a lucid dream. The following is a case from one of our subjects which illustrates the difficulty which can be experienced in switching on an electric light to realistic effect in a false awakening. In this case, incidentally, the difficulty seems to have been one of the factors leading to lucidity.

> Appear to wake up in bed normally. Try to turn on bedside light but it won't work. Feeling very groggy. Get up and try to turn on main light. That won't work either. Then go through to kitchen to try to turn on that light. Same story. Think that maybe metered electricity has run out and think of going to look in cupboard with torch, but also start to suspect that this is a dream. Surroundings dark (but lighter than they would be if all lights were really off).
>
> (Subject N.C.)

In an experiment carried out by Dr Keith Hearne eight habitual lucid dreamers were asked to make deliberate experiments with light switches while in a lucid dream (Hearne, 1981). Only one found it possible to perform the task of switching on the light. It is interesting to note that the one subject who succeeded at the task found that she could only do so by covering her eyes in the dream, which abolished her previous imagery. Two typical quotations from subjects who experienced difficulty with the task were as follows.

I switched it on and off several times and looked up at the light, which was a naked bulb. It kept sparking and flickering – I could see the filament light up and glow orangy-red. I thought 'typical of this place, nothing works properly'.

I went to the bedroom light switch and turned it on. To my surprise, a light came on behind me in a room to the side, but not in the bedroom. Then I tried the kitchen light switch. Nothing happened.

Another of Hearne's subjects reported that it was possible to switch a light off first, and then on, but not the other way round.

The light switch phenomenon might suggest that there is a difficulty in simulating sufficient intensity of 'illumination' in the dream imagery to mimic the effect of an electric light. However, this seems unlikely to be the explanation of the effect, since lucid dreams are sometimes described as brilliantly or even dazzlingly illuminated, and certainly lucid dreamers have the experience of walking around rooms where the electric lighting is on.

Another possible hypothesis is that the difficulty is that of producing extreme variations in the apparent level of illumination, rather than that of producing a particular level of brightness *per se*. Again, this explanation does not fit with the reported characteristics of lucid dreams, since not only are they sometimes described as being very bright, but extremes of contrast are occasionally reported in them. For example, one subject suggests that what triggered her lucidity in a certain dream may have been the extreme brightness of the scene (a brilliantly sunlit canal), or the contrast with dark streets just before; the subject describes this as an impossible contrast by normal standards.

Hearne (1990) regards the light switch phenomenon as a universal feature of lucid dreams. His explanation of the effect is that dream imagery has a physiologically determined ceiling limit for brightness at any given moment, though this ceiling value may vary over time. There does not, however, seem to be any independent evidence for this hypothesis, apart from the light switch phenomenon which it is invoked to explain, so it appears to us to be a little *ad hoc*. Moreover, since Hearne made his study, a single experienced lucid dreamer, Kenneth Moss, has reported that he was able to perform the light switch test successfully in eleven out of fifteen lucid dreams in which he made the experiment (Moss, 1989). Moss reports various methods which he believes facilitate successful performance of the task, such as finding an angle of view which includes both the light switch and the light source in close proximity to each other in the visual field.

Examples such as that of Dr Moss suggest that lucid dreamers do not necessarily all experience an inherent difficulty in bringing about a sudden change to a high degree of apparent brightness. It may be that the difficulty resides, at least in part, in the fact that the relationship between the operation of a light switch and the level of illumination produced by an electric light bulb is something that is learnt and fully understood at a relatively late stage in development and at a relatively conscious level.

In support of such an interpretation we would point out that covering the eyes with the hands usually has the effect, in lucid dreams, of obliterating the previous imagery, and reproducing the blackness which would result from cutting off normal vision in waking life. There would seem, therefore, to be no absolute difficulty in reproducing sudden transitions from light to dark and back again. The difference between the two situations may be that we all become familiar from birth with the effect associated with closing and re-opening the eyes, whereas the switch–illumination effect is one learned relatively late in life and hence does not produce so automatic an expectation.

We mentioned that Dr Hearne's one subject who succeeded in switching on the light did so after covering her eyes with her hands. As discussed in the previous chapter, this technique seems useful more generally in bringing about changes of scenery in lucid dreams. Sudden and complete changes of scene appear to be difficult to effect otherwise; if the dreamer tries to bring such changes about, it seems that the dream tends to proceed towards the desired end by some uncertain process of gradual development. An example of this process would be a case quoted by Green (1968a, p. 103), in which a lucid dreamer decided that he would prefer to be in a glass-house at Kew Gardens, rather than travelling on the London Underground as he seemed to be doing at the time. The result of his concentrating on this idea was that the roof of the carriage began to look dome-like and semi-transparent, and his fellow passengers began to sprout twigs and leaves. Cases such as this suggest that what lucid dreams find it difficult to produce is not just discontinuities related to the level of brightness, but sudden and total discontinuities of any kind, at least if the corresponding ones in waking life are not familiar to us from the most basic stages of development. One might say that lucid dream imagery seems to 'prefer' to proceed by evolution rather than revolution.

Chapter 11

Methods of inducing lucid dreams

It sometimes happens that people who have never before had lucid dreams start to do so as soon as they become aware of the idea. A number of our subjects have said that they had their first lucid dream after reading *Lucid Dreams* (Green, 1968a), and some researchers who became engaged in studying the subject from an academic point of view found that they themselves started to have them. For those who wish to start developing lucid dreams, a simple prescription, which may be sufficient, is to think about the idea of lucid dreaming before falling asleep each night. Some people keep a book about lucid dreaming by their bedside and read part of it each night to focus their mind on the idea.

It now seems fairly well established that the morning is the most favourable time for the occurrence of lucid dreaming (Green, 1968a; LaBerge, 1988b). Several practitioners therefore favour performing some mental exercise when they first wake, designed to focus their mind on the intention to dream lucidly, and then falling asleep again. Stephen LaBerge would ask himself immediately on waking, 'What was I dreaming?' Then he would go over in his mind the dream which he had just had, and say to himself, as he fell asleep again, 'Next time I'm dreaming, I want to remember to recognise I'm dreaming'. He would then visualise himself in the previous dream he had just memorised, only this time as a lucid dream in which he was aware that he was dreaming, as he went through the sequence of dream events. Although the next dream that arose might be quite different from the preceding one, he found that this procedure considerably increased his chances of becoming lucid in it (LaBerge, 1985).

Some other lucid dreamers have found it helpful to get out of bed for a short time when they first wake in the morning and engage in a preferred activity before returning to bed. One of our subjects reads a book for a short time to ensure mental alertness. Other dreamers may write down a previous dream or meditate before going back to sleep.

The development of lucid dreams is one area in which considerable progress has been made since the publication of *Lucid Dreams* (see Price and Cohen, 1988, for a review of this area). It has now been shown that it is possible for motivated people to increase their lucid dream frequency very considerably. Stephen LaBerge mentions two students who improved from a frequency of fewer than one per month to twenty a month. Paul Tholey claims that virtually all subjects should be able to develop lucid dreams by his techniques, probably within weeks and certainly within months. We shall focus on four relatively distinct processes which are advocated by one or more practitioners as facilitating lucidity.

The first of these is the habit of recalling one's non-lucid dreams on waking; it appears that this in itself may facilitate the occurrence of lucid ones. If one's recall of non-lucid dreams is initially poor, one may be able to improve it by practice. As with lucid dreams themselves, the mere intention to remember one's non-lucid dreams may be sufficient to bring about some improvement. In addition, the habit should be cultivated of remembering the dream one was just having as a first reaction to finding oneself awake. The dream should be recalled as far as possible before one allows other trains of thought to arise. Recording one's dreams in writing as soon as one has remembered as much of them as possible is also helpful in developing the ability to remember dreams more completely.

The second line of approach concerns the hypnagogic state. Various methods of passing directly from waking into lucidly dreaming sleep without the loss of conscious awareness have been described, beginning with the Tibetan Buddhists of the eighth century, according to Gillespie (1988). The simplest of these methods is to watch one's own mind as one falls asleep, as advocated by Ouspensky (1960). The idea is to retain critical self-awareness while watching dreaming associations and images as they start to arise. By practising this technique it is eventually possible for some people to pass directly into the dream scenery without losing awareness of its status.

Stephen LaBerge advocates occupying the mind with

mechanical tasks while falling asleep, as if to preserve a central alertness while the rest of the mind becomes engaged in dreaming. Or the subject may mentally repeat to himself a reminder that he is to notice he is dreaming. LaBerge repeated to himself, 'One, this is a dream, two, this is a dream, three, this is a dream,' and so on, until a dream had actually arisen in his mind, and he realised that it had done so.

Interestingly, subjects who have failed at the task of remaining lucid while falling asleep have nevertheless found that the attempt may have the effect of causing lucidity to arise in another dream later in the night.

Apart from falling asleep with one's mind focused on the intention of achieving lucidity, whether by repeating to oneself an autosuggestion or simply by observing the contents of one's mind with this intention, the most effective technique for inducing lucid dreams is probably to cultivate a constantly critical and questioning attitude of mind towards the state in which one finds oneself. This is the third method which we shall discuss.

Our Subject E describes as follows the importance of thinking about lucid dreaming in the waking state as an aid to future lucidity.

> Another factor favouring lucid dreaming is one's attitude to the question while awake. Thus if one concentrates on the idea that during dreams awareness of the fact will arise, resolving to respond to any incongruity by considering whether one may be dreaming – then this seems to penetrate into the unconscious mind with the desired effect. A similar thing is true of reflections as to why one failed on a particular occasion to consider the question deeply enough (perhaps without realising it at the time). Then on subsequent occasions one tends to recall these reflections.

If one is in the habit of examining one's situation in waking life and asking oneself questions about its status, it seems that eventually one is likely to do the same thing within a dream. One way of regarding this phenomenon is to see it as an illustration of Freud's idea of 'day-residues' – that one tends to dream about whatever has happened during the preceding waking day.

Paul Tholey considers the technique to be particularly effective in the case of subjects who have not previously had lucid dreams. He recommends that a subject wishing to have lucid dreams should ask himself 'Am I dreaming or not?' at least five to ten times a day, each time accustoming himself to think critically about the question and to examine any features of his surroundings and mental state which might give him clues. First, he should try to imagine that he is dreaming at the present time and that everything he perceives, including his own body, is illusory. Are there any features around him which are not appropriate to a waking situation? Then the subject should test his memory of recent events. What was he doing before his present activity or occupation? If he is walking, where has he come from? And what happened before that? Can he remember getting up in the morning? Can he remember what he did yesterday? If this examination of recent memory is carried out in a dream it will often quickly come to a halt, as the events of a dream do not go far into the past. Practising the memory check in the waking state, as with other checks of environment and sensation, increases the likelihood that the dreamer will find himself carrying out the same check in a dream.

The question concerning dreaming should be asked, and the checks made, as often as possible, and it is particularly helpful to associate this practice with events which are characteristic of dreams, such as anything surprising or improbable, or the experiencing of strong emotions. This will form an association between the occurrence of anything at all out of the ordinary and the asking of the question.

The fourth approach is really a sub-variety of the third, and consists of carrying out specific 'tests' such as one might perform in the pre-lucid state to determine one's condition, only in waking life. Thus the subject may make a resolution to carry out some particular action to test the dream state, and carrying out this check could be incorporated as part of his waking routine whenever he asks himself the question, 'Am I dreaming now?'. For example, he might try to push his way through a wall, or to pick up an object which he knows is in reality too heavy for him to lift, to see whether the results of this attempt are as they are usually expected to be. Picking up a book to see whether it is as easy as usual to read might also be used as a test, in view of the difficulty that this task sometimes presents in lucid dreams.

The idea seems to be that, if one is regularly performing such 'tests' during waking life, then one is more likely to find oneself doing something similar in a dream, and possibly become lucid as a consequence, because the test gives an abnormal result in the dream state.

It is an interesting question to what extent the process of 'learning' to have lucid dreams can be assimilated to psychological ideas of conditioning. In the classical conditioning experiments of Pavlov (1960) using dogs as subjects, the 'unconditioned stimulus', the smell of food, which gave rise to the 'unconditioned response' of salivation, was preceded or accompanied by the 'conditioned stimulus', a bell tone, over a number of trials until eventually the bell alone was sufficient to produce salivation even in the absence of the smell of food. Salivation thus became a 'conditioned' response. An essential element in this situation was the reward of actual food following on the presentation of the bell tone; at least in a certain proportion of the trials. The food thus acts as the 'reinforcer', strengthening the connection between bell and salivation.

The straitjacket of this rather mechanical model of learning has been loosened somewhat by more recent theorists of conditioning, who are prepared to allow that internal states of the organism, or even 'cognitive events', can themselves act as conditioned stimuli. Dream events would presumably be allowed to fall into such a category. In the case of subjects who initially become lucid spontaneously, say as a result of a nightmare, or in response to some incongruity in the dream situation, we could think of the question 'Could this be a dream?' as an unconditioned response to the events in the dream. The achievement of insight certainly fits the role of a 'reinforcer', since it seems to be intrinsically pleasurable, even in instances in which it is not immediately preceded by a nightmare which it relieves.

The various 'training' methods described in this chapter could perhaps be viewed as attempts to condition this ordinarily unconditioned insight response to new stimuli that might arise in the dream state. For example, if the subject follows Tholey's advice and tries to think 'Could this be a dream?' whenever anything stressful or surprising occurs in waking life, then the question may occur to him or her as a conditioned response to stressful or surprising situations in dreams. The 'conditioned stimulus' need not even be anything like the sort of dream occurrences which most commonly give rise to spontaneous lucidity in dreams. The subject could simply pick any stimulus which he or she thinks occurs quite commonly in his non-lucid dreams, or which might be made so to occur by experimental manipulation in waking life. Thus the subject might put, say, a green watering can in the hall of his house and think about the question of whether he might be dreaming whenever he walked past it. On Freud's principle of day-residues, this might increase the likelihood of the subject dreaming of green watering cans and, it might be hoped, of 'responding' with the associated question.

The methods for facilitating lucid dreams which we have described in this chapter are intended as pragmatic suggestions for people wishing to induce lucidity in themselves rather than as established research findings. It should be noted that the techniques developed so far have yet to be validated in controlled studies involving reasonable numbers of subjects. The researchers who have evolved them have usually been expert lucid dreamers themselves, and it is easy to fall into the trap of generalising in too optimistic a way from one's own experience, as we have noted with regard to the scepticism with which some have regarded the possibility of lucid dreaming. The subjects who have applied their techniques have been small in number and presumably self-selecting, or at any rate not necessarily representative of the population at large. There is also the possibility that the success which has been reported by subjects to the originators of the techniques may owe something to their having had personal contact with the relevant originator. It seems to be a feature of psychotherapeutic techniques that they work best when communicated directly to patients by their originators, who presumably believe in them most strongly and convey their confidence and enthusiasm to their patients. It is possible that a similar effect might operate in the case of lucid dream induction techniques. This is not to say that any of them are ineffective, only that there is a need for controlled studies on a group level if we are to make reliable observations.

In addition, we feel that the question of individual differences has been relatively neglected so far in research into techniques for facilitating lucid dreams. We think it possible that such individual differences may eventually be found to play a considerable role in the ease with which people are able to develop lucidity in dreams. A notable example of someone who apparently found the task extremely difficult is the nineteenth-century poet and classical scholar F. W. H. Myers, who was one of the founders of the Society for Psychical Research. One of his experiences is quoted and discussed at various points in *Lucid Dreams*. Myers writes that he only achieved lucidity on three occasions out of a total of 3,000 nights (Myers, 1887). LaBerge (1988a) comments that Myers 'may serve as a reminder of the fact that what is needed is not "painstaking", but effective effort.' While this may be true, we think that long-term dispositional factors may also play a role in a case like Myers'. We suggest that any learned training procedure needs for its maximum effect to fall on the receptive ground of a particular type of nervous system. In Chapter 15 of this book, we will argue that the type of nervous system in question is one that is characterised by relative lability of arousal, so that it is more liable than average to enter a state of unusually high arousal during sleep. On this basis one would predict that people who score highly on scales designed to measure lability of arousal, such as the Hypomania scale of Eckblad and Chapman (1986), will be more successful in the application of lucidity induction techniques than people whose level of arousal is relatively stable and who score modestly on scales such as the Hypomania.

Predictions of this kind could be tested by applying a standardised lucidity induction programme to a group of subjects whose scores on questionnaire measures had already been determined, and seeing if these scores correlated with some objective measure of relative success at achieving lucidity, such as the length of time before the first lucid dream, frequency of lucid dreaming thereafter, and so on.

Finally, we would mention that we are sometimes asked whether there are any risks attached to lucid dreaming. The sorts of dangers people have in mind seem to be of two different kinds. The first concerns what might be called after-effects, both short- and long-term. The short-term effect of a negative kind that is most often suggested is something akin to sleep deprivation, since the lucid dreamer may not have had the normal amount of restful, 'unconscious' sleep; and a long-term effect sometimes suggested is a loss of interest in the affairs of everyday life, due to the absorbing interest of the lucid dream state. We shall be discussing both these possibilities in more detail in Chapter 14, but we will anticipate the conclusion of that discussion here, which is that there is, as far as we know, no evidence that either of these dangers has been realised in any particular case, although this does not of course mean that they could not be so in the future.

As regards more immediate dangers inherent in the state of lucidity in dreams, we have been asked whether there is a risk of 'bad trips', analogous to those sometimes reported by users of psychedelic drugs. Again, we can only say that we do not know of any such experiences, and a priori we do not find it easy to envisage how such a situation could arise, since the manipulation of the subject's mental state takes place purely on an internal level, and not by external means, as in recreational drug use. Nor is there any evidence as yet that the state differs in any extreme way, physiologically, from that of non-lucid REM sleep. No one, for example, has yet reported spontaneous hyperventilation (over-breathing) in lucid dreamers, such as has been implicated in the phenomenon of panic attacks.

At the same time we would be the first to recognise that the fact that something has not occurred in the past is no guarantee that it will not occur in the future. We therefore suggest that the description of other people's techniques for facilitating lucidity which we have described in this chapter should be taken as just that – a description, for the benefit of anyone who has already decided on his or her own responsibility that they wish to take advantage of such suggestions, and not in any sense an encouragement that they should do so, or an endorsement of the efficacy or absolute safety of any possible outcome.

The most negative phenomenon we have come across in connection with lucid dreaming is the experience of claustrophobia, which we have dealt with in earlier chapters, and which may concern either the intellectual possibility of not waking up, or in some cases the actual inability to do so despite conscious efforts. As we have seen, the latter variant of the phenomenon is not peculiar to lucid dreams, but occurs in connection with sleep paralysis as well.

Having discussed the possibility of negative experiences and effects in connection with lucid dreaming, we think it is appropriate to move on to discuss the possible beneficial effects of cultivating lucidity in dreams, and we will do this in Chapters 12 and 13.

Chapter 12

Lucid dreams and the treatment of nightmares

Among inexperienced lucid dreamers, a common situation in which lucidity arises seems to be that in which the dreamer recognises that he is having a nightmare, or a dream with unpleasant elements, and makes use of his recognition of the situation to turn the nightmare into a less unpleasant dream or to awaken from it. People who learn to control their dreams in this way may, however, have only very brief periods of lucid dreaming in the process, and it may never occur to them that this might be developed or extended.

The fact that escaping from nightmares may occur before any more elaborate development of lucid dreams for their own sake is illustrated by the following extract from one of the early writers on lucid dreams, Oliver Fox, who was working at a time when there was no general appreciation of the possibility of developing lucidity in dreams. Fox's remarks show that lucidity in response to nightmares occurred in his case before he became an experienced lucid dreamer. It is also of interest that Fox suggests that it is the stress of nightmares which may be one of the operative factors linking them to the increased likelihood of lucidity occurring. Subsequent research may be seen as relevant to this speculation in two respects. First, lucid dreams have been found to be predominantly associated with 'paradoxical' or rapid eye movement (REM) phases of sleep, which, at least as regards cortical activity, may be regarded as a relatively aroused form of sleep. Secondly, there is some indication that spontaneous lucidity is more likely to arise following days of relatively high arousal in the subject's waking life (Gackenbach et al., 1983). We shall discuss the significance of these findings, and the role of arousal in general in relation to lucid dreams, more fully in Chapter 15.

I observed that sometimes in a nightmare, or a painful dream of the ordinary non-celestial kind, the very unpleasantness of my predicament would give rise to the thoughts: 'But this can't be real! This wouldn't happen to me! I must be dreaming!' And then: 'I've had enough of this. I'm going to wake up.' And I would promptly escape from the situation by, as it were, pushing the dream aside and waking. In those days I never realised the great possibilities latent in this discovery, but my curiosity was aroused to some extent. I wondered why it was only now and then one could get to know *in the dream* that it was a dream, and how was this knowledge acquired? . . . It is interesting to note that while many people can escape from a nightmare in this way, very few know they are dreaming if the dream is pleasant or ordinary. It may be that it is the intense emotional *stress* which aroused the critical faculty in the consciousness, enabling it to argue from the extraordinary circumstances of the dream that they are too far removed from everyday life to be real.

(Fox, 1962, p. 30)

Hervey de Saint-Denys describes how he managed to release himself from a recurrent nightmare by developing lucidity. At one stage in his life he used to find himself dreaming of fleeing from dreadful monsters through an endless series of rooms. He struggled to open each door as he came to it, and heard behind him the bloodcurdling cries of the monsters, which seemed to be gaining on him. After a nightmare of this sort he would awake panting and sweating. These dreams seemed to be becoming more frequent, as finding himself in a room in his dreams seemed to suggest to him the dreaded monsters, and when the thought arose they actually appeared. Finally, in one such experience the recurrent situation made him aware that he was dreaming, and instead of attempting to run from the monsters he set his back to a wall, determined to confront his pursuers.

I stared at my principal assailant. He bore some resemblance to one of those bristling and grimacing demons which are sculptured on cathedral porches. Academic curiosity soon overcame all my other emotions. I saw the fantastic monster halt a few paces from me, hissing and leaping about. Once I had mastered my fear his actions appeared merely burlesque. I noticed the claws on one of his hands, or paws, I should say.

There were seven in all, each very precisely delineated. The monster's features were all precise and realistic: hair and eyebrows, what looked like a wound on his shoulder, and many other details. . . . The result of concentrating my attention on this figure was that all his acolytes vanished, as if by magic. Soon the leading monster also began to slow down, lose precision, and take on a downy appearance. He finally changed into a sort of floating hide, which resembled the faded costumes used as street-signs by fancy-dress shops at carnival time.

(Hervey de Saint-Denys, 1867, quoted in McCreery, 1973, pp. 102–4)

Hervey de Saint-Denys used no special technique to try to ensure that his recurrent nightmares would make him aware of his situation. A modern dreamer with the same problem might repeat to himself frequently in waking life some verbal formula such as 'Rooms – monsters – I am dreaming', until the verbal association took effect within his dream.

Patricia Garfield describes a somewhat similar response to a recurrent nightmare, in which she also turns and confronts her pursuers. In this instance there is no clear indication in the account that the dream became lucid, but the result appears to have been beneficial nevertheless.

As part of a long dream story, my youngest daughter and I are being chased by a gang of guys who intend to rape us. This is a recurrent dream image for me, resulting from an actual experience at about age thirteen when I was chased through the woods by a gang of boys who said, 'Get her!' and from whom I barely escaped by running to my grandmother's backyard where she happily was within sight and earshot. In the dream:

. . . we round a corner and see that the guys have blocked off the hallway and about six of them wait with their arms apart to grab us. I say, 'Oh, no,' and we turn and run. As I am desperately running, I suddenly realize I'm not supposed to do that. I stop myself and, with a feeling of great effort, yet certain I must do it, say, 'Come on!' and force myself to turn round and face them. Then we are fighting them. We pinch and pull and hit. Suddenly I have something I am spraying in their eyes. In a few minutes we have successfully fought them off.

(Garfield, 1974, p. 101)

It would appear from the last two examples that dreamers who become lucid in their nightmares may find it desirable to adopt a positive attitude towards any dream assailant. Monsters should be faced with compassion and acceptance rather than fear, and pursuers should be confronted and counter-attacked. However, as we mentioned in Chapter 5, it is characteristic of lucid dreams that unpleasant emotional elements tend to be absent from them, and the realisation of dreaming is in itself usually sufficient for the previously non-lucid dream to lose its nightmarish quality.

Release from nightmares is one of the most obviously useful applications of lucid dreaming, and it might be considered in the context of treatment for people suffering from post-traumatic stress disorder in which the sufferer is sometimes tormented by recurrent bad dreams after hijacks and similar traumatic experiences.

LUCID DREAMING IN CHILDREN

As long ago as 1921 Mary Arnold-Forster suggested that lucid dream techniques should be used to relieve the sufferings of children, some of whom are considerably harrowed by their liability to unpleasant dreams (Arnold-Forster, 1921). Certainly, lucid dreams have been reported as occurring to children as young as 5 years old, and this seems an interesting and possibly fruitful field for further research.

The following is a lucid dream recorded in adult life by our Subject B. He believes he was about 5 at the time of this experience.

At the time we were living in a country cottage with a thatched roof and stone floors. I found myself dreaming that I was in the living room of this cottage, and knew that I was dreaming. I was surprised by the realism and lack of distortion of everything. Usually I felt my dreams were unpleasantly vague and grotesque, but this was not. I noticed the sunlight on the motes of dust in the air. Pallas Athene was there, standing in the air in front of me, and I admired the aesthetic qualities of her figure, which was clearly defined, well-proportioned and with convincing texture. It was aesthetically pleasing, in white and gold, in fact quite an ideal representation of what I thought such a figure should be. She presented me with a flower in a pot, which I accepted as seemed appropriate. It was quite common in my books of myths and legends for goddesses to show their favour by presenting useful things. After this I think the dream stopped being lucid, or became less so, and turned into a confused kind of hide-and-seek in the woods at the back of the cottage, including myself, my parents, and a red dwarf, who wished to steal my flower-pot.

It is interesting to consider what differences there may be between the lucid dreams of children and adults. The last example suggests that at least in certain cases young children may have much the same experience as adults of a critical attention to the dream and an appreciation of the quality and detail of the images represented.

Another of the Institute's habitual lucid dreamers, Subject E, describes her childhood experience of lucidity as follows:

As a child I would sometimes realise that I was dreaming just prior to waking; so real did the dream-objects appear that it almost seemed possible to bring them back into the waking world by holding on to them. By the time I was in my teens awareness of dreaming was occurring in deeper states of sleep, sometimes in association with gliding or floating episodes.

The following account is from another of our subjects, a Dane writing in English.

The first lucid dream I remember having was when I was only 7 years of age.

First I had an ordinary dream of which I don't remember much. By the end of this I was together with a schoolfellow in my playing room, when I suddenly realised that I was dreaming.

I therefore said to my friend: 'Hey, wait a minute – we're dreaming!' He seemed to ignore what I had just said, so I went to my mother who was sitting in the living-room. When I told her what I had just told my playmate, her reaction was just the same as his.

Naturally their reactions were rather annoying, but I didn't become angry. Instead a sensation of wonder and a feeling of possessing superior knowledge overwhelmed me. Then I went to the windows which were covered by drapes, and shouted out loud: 'So you don't believe me! Well, then look for yourself!' And while saying this I pulled down the curtains.

Outside was a scenery quite different from that of the 'real' world: a small village in the most beautiful colours, and covered with tinsel. All the buildings seemed to be glowing. I could see a church and also hear the sound of church bells.

It was a very beautiful sight and the mood of the situation felt so nice, so I didn't hesitate to jump out of the window and into the village.

At this point my grandmother woke me up, since it was time for me to get ready to go to school. The time must have been about 8.00 a.m.

(Subject O.D.)

From an evidential point of view, a weakness in all the cases we have quoted is that they were only written down many years after the event, and it is not possible to assess the extent to which the subjects' memories may have been modified or distorted with the passage of time. However, there does not seem to be any reason in principle why children should not write contemporaneous accounts of any lucid dream experiences they may have, and this is something that might be encouraged in any suitable subject in future research.

As yet, it is not possible to say much about the most effective techniques that might be used in relieving childhood nightmares through the cultivation of lucidity, as the idea is applied only sporadically in individual cases, though apparently sometimes quite successfully, as in the following instance.

Once, when I was making long-distance small-talk with my niece, I brought out my favourite hobby-horse and inquired, 'How are your dreams lately?' Madeleina, then seven years old, burst out with the description of a fearful nightmare. She had dreamed that she had gone swimming, as she often did, in the local reservoir. But this time, she had been threatened and terrified by a little-girl-eating shark! I sympathised with her fear and added matter of factly, 'But of course you know there aren't *really* any sharks in Colorado.' She replied, 'Of course not!' So I continued, 'Well, since you know there aren't really any sharks where you swim, if you ever see one there again, it would be because you were *dreaming*. And, of course, a dream shark can't really do you any harm. It's only frightening if you don't know that it's a dream. But once you *do* know that you're dreaming, you can do whatever you like – you could even make friends with the dream shark, if you wanted to! Why not give it a try?' Madeleina seemed intrigued and soon proved that she had bitten the bait. A week later, she telephoned to announce proudly, 'Do you know what I did? *I rode on the back of the shark!'*

(LaBerge, 1985, p. 182)

This type of treatment certainly appears to be a promising area of development, and it seems likely that research would help to delineate the most effective methods for use with children.

Stephen LaBerge has drawn attention to an interesting historical example of someone using lucidity to counteract nightmares, in the form of a letter written in 1779 by the philosopher, Thomas Reid. As a youth Reid was apparently plagued by nightmares, which not only disturbed his sleep, but left a 'disagreeable impression' on him the next day. Finally it occurred to him that

it was worth trying whether it was possible to recollect that it was all a dream, and that I was in no real danger. I often went to sleep with my mind as strongly impressed as I could with this thought, that I never in my lifetime was in any real danger, and that every fright I had was a dream. After many fruitless endeavors to recollect this when the danger appeared, I effected it at last, and have often, when I was sliding over a precipice into the abyss, recollected that it was all a dream, and boldly jumped down. The effect of this commonly was that I immediately awoke. But I awoke calm and intrepid, which I thought a greater acquisition. . . . After this my dreams were never uneasy.

(Seafield, 1865, p. 194; quoted in LaBerge, 1988a)

There are two points in this passage which show a striking resemblance to more modern accounts. The first is the fact that Reid's lucidity usually led to waking. We remarked at the start of this chapter that people who only experience lucidity arising out of nightmares often report only brief periods of lucid dreaming. The second point is that Reid seems to have arrived independently at one of the methods of lucid dream induction described in the previous chapter, namely that of trying while falling asleep to keep in mind the intention to achieve insight later in the night.

LUCID DREAMING AND PSYCHOPATHOLOGY

It is possible that the cultivation of lucidity in dreams might be of benefit to schizophrenics in some cases. A number of studies have suggested that the dreams of schizophrenics are particularly liable to include aggressive or threatening elements. Robbins (1988), reviewing these studies, writes:

> The dreams of schizophrenics are fraught with anxiety-provoking situations. We all have these experiences occasionally in dreams, but in the schizophrenic they seem to be running rampant. It is as if the control mechanisms that protect us from being overwhelmed by anxiety have gone out of kilter. One has a sense of floodgates that do not work.
>
> (Robbins, 1988, p. 64)

In the case of a schizophrenic person feeling out of control of various aspects of his or her mental life, it is possible that the experience of gaining control over at least one of them, namely distressing dreams, might have a generalised therapeutic effect, quite apart from the localised relief that might be obtained for the particular symptom. We shall be discussing two non-schizophrenic subjects who claim to have found that the experience of control in lucid dreams had a beneficial 'carry-over' effect on them in waking life in Chapter 13.

It is also conceivable that the cultivation of lucid dreams might have prophylactic value. Hartmann *et al.* (1981) studied a group of thirty-eight respondents to a Boston newspaper advertisement for people who suffered from nightmares at least once a week, and found a strikingly raised incidence of psychopathology, both among the subjects themselves and their relatives. (Similar advertisements for subjects for drug and insomnia studies did not produce the same result.) The authors went so far as to suggest that a child's continuing to have frequent nightmares at the age of, say, 10 to 12, i.e. several years beyond the age at which such experiences usually tend to diminish, might have predictive value as a marker of risk for schizophrenia. However, if such children could be taught to develop lucidity in dreams, it is conceivable that this might even reduce the risk of breakdown in later life.

Brylowski (1990) considers that 'the symptom of nightmares cuts across diagnostic boundaries' and cites evidence of a raised incidence of nightmares in other diagnostic categories beside schizophrenia, such as alcohol dependency and drug abuse. He describes a considerable degree of success in treating frequent nightmares (one to four a week) through the cultivating of lucidity in a 35-year-old female patient with a diagnosis of borderline personality disorder[1] and major depression. There was a history of childhood abuse by her father. She was instructed to keep a dream/nightmare journal and was given LaBerge's book *Lucid Dreaming* (1985) to read, as well as having the concept of lucidity in dreams explained to her by the therapist. Over a six-month period, which included twenty-four sessions with the therapist, the subject reported three lucid dreams, the first occurring between the third and fourth session. Two of the lucid dreams seem to have arisen out of nightmare situations. The treatment seems to have to a considerable extent 'defused' the situation with regard to the particular symptom of nightmares. Brylowski writes that 'the emerging ability in lucid dream skills allowed for mastery of negative affect while the nightmare was still occurring and awakening in a more positive affective state. . . . Her emotional response shifted from terror to expectant curiosity' (1991, p. 81). He also considered that the success in treating the nightmares carried over into other aspects of the subject's life. As he puts it: 'when dealing with a torrent of stirred emotions [in waking life], the patient's memory of recent emotional dream situations in which she had successfully mastered her reactions reinforced the notion that she had the capacity to do the same with waking circumstances' (ibid.).

This was a case study involving a single subject, so clearly one cannot conclude too much from it, but it does seem to support the notion put forward above that the development of lucidity in dreams as a strategy for coping with nighmares might have beneficial effects that could spread to other areas of the subject's life. In any controlled study of the benefits of lucid dreaming, in areas other than the specific symptom of nightmares, there would of course be considerable methodological difficulties in separating out the effects of developing lucidity from any other therapeutic effort that was being undertaken at the time, and it is recognised by Brylowski in relation to his particular patient that 'it is difficult to attribute direct cause and effect between changes in dream life and in real life'. However, this is a sort of difficulty that is encountered in the assessment of any sort of psychological therapy. The effect of a convincing display of concern and attention from a therapist is hard to quantify and is likely to be involved in the application of any particular technique. To control for it requires the same therapist to apply in a relatively disinterested manner different techniques on two or more independent groups of subjects, which may raise ethical issues, as well as being difficult to carry out in practice if the therapist actually has a prior opinion as to their relative efficacy. However, such general theoretical difficulties need not be an obstacle to the practical application of lucid dreaming to the treatment of nightmares considered as a specific symptom.

Chapter 13

Other therapeutic implications of lucid dreaming

LUCID DREAMS IN PSYCHOTHERAPY

A number of people, including certain psychotherapists, have believed that lucid dreams may be of use in helping to resolve psychological problems. Research on psychotherapeutic applications of lucid dreaming is, however, still at a very early stage. Not surprisingly, therefore, a variety of different approaches have been used in the attempt to utilise lucid dreaming for this purpose (see Gackenbach and LaBerge, 1988, for various articles on this topic).

One subject known to the present authors has told us that he has solved his psychological problems, at least in part, by having the experience of control which lucid dreams represented, and that this feeling of being in control of his own life had carried over to the waking state. A similar position is held by the psychotherapist Kenneth Kelzer, author of a book about his own lucid dream experiences entitled *The Sun and the Shadow* (Kelzer, 1987). The following extract from one of his articles illustrates his point of view, which places emphasis on spiritual development. Describing one of his early lucid dreams which might have developed into a nightmare, Kelzer writes:

> [I]n the moment that I became lucid I experienced total inner transformation. All my fear vanished in an instant, and inside of myself I felt full of courage. Complete clarity of vision in this dream yielded instant transformation. This became one of the important principles that I learned from this particular lucid dream. To see fully is to have courage. To see fully is to have no fear. But, as is so evident when we examine our world, we human beings seldom see anything fully in our normal state of

consciousness. More often than not, as the apostle Paul wrote: 'We see now through a glass, darkly, but then we shall see face to face.'

One of the purposes of lucid dreaming, I am now convinced, is to give people the experience, however fleeting or temporary, of spiritual and psychological mastery. These tastes of mastery and moments of transformation spur us on to continue the inward journey.

(Kelzer, 1987)

Kelzer is certainly among those who take an extreme view of the potentialities for the extension of consciousness which lucid dreams may have. However, not all lucid dreamers, even practised ones, have had what the American psychologist Abraham Maslow called 'peak experiences' (Maslow, 1962) in their lucid dreams as Kelzer claims to have had, and Kelzer seems to be describing something very different to what one usually thinks of as a lucid dream when he writes:

In this dream I experienced a lucidity that was so vastly different and beyond the range of anything I had previously encountered. At this point I prefer to apply the concept of the spectrum of consciousness to the lucid dream and assert that within the lucid state a person may have access to a spectrum or range of psychic energy that is so vast, so broad and so unique as to defy classification.

(Kelzer, 1987)

A possibility that seems to occur to a number of lucid dreamers, and which may possibly have therapeutic implications, is that they may perform actions with impunity in their lucid dreams which would be unacceptable in waking life, thus perhaps relieving certain frustrations. For example, Ann Faraday, a dream researcher and hypnotherapist trained in Freudian analysis, recounts the following dream. As mentioned in Chapter 9 on control of lucid dreams, this example may in fact be somewhat unusual in that the dreamer appears to be relatively free of any inhibition about seeming to 'physically' damage a person in her dream:

I dreamed I was having dinner with a rather uptight group of psychologists when a woman across the table suddenly started recriminating with me for leaving the world of the academic elite and lowering my standards to those of the Sunday newspapers. I protested that this was an exaggeration, and that I believed the layman was entitled to at least some of our ideas, especially as he was paying for our research. At this she literally spat across the table that I was bringing the whole profession into disrepute, that we must retain some vestige of authority, and so on. My fury rose to such a pitch that I had an irresistible desire to beat her up, and no sooner had I become aware of this desire than I realized with the utmost clarity that I was dreaming and could do exactly what I wanted because dream bodies cannot get hurt.

So, leaning across the table, I grabbed her by the hair, punched her face, and knocked her front teeth out. This inspired me to further violence and with an exhilaration I have never previously experienced I dragged her onto the floor and began to beat up her body in the same way. Of course, she fought back, and I can still feel the slashing of her fingernails across my cheek and the kicks of what felt like hobnailed boots on my back. At last I detected the waning of her strength, and the fight was over. Then the scene changed, and I found myself in another room walking toward this woman, who was now transformed and wearing a nurse's uniform. As we approached each other, I reminded myself that I must not magically change the events of my lucid dream but allow them to happen spontaneously and observe the outcome. I noted that she was smiling now and that her front teeth were back in place. She then put out her arms to me in a friendly gesture, and we hugged each other.

I woke up with a great sense of well-being, as if my humanistic underdog had really made its protest against my academic topdog. . . . I felt it not just in my mind but throughout my whole body.

(Faraday, 1972, p. 310)

We do not consider that there is as yet much evidence that proceedings of this kind have beneficial effects, or indeed that lucid dreaming in general represents a useful tool for psychotherapists, except in the limited context of nightmare treatment discussed in Chapter 12. On the other hand, one should not be surprised that the situation concerning the therapeutic effects of lucid dreams is in general so uncertain, when one considers that the effects of psychotherapy in the waking state are still not a matter of universal agreement (see, for example, Masson, 1990 for a critical review). This is despite the fact that psychotherapeutic techniques have by now been used, over a period of nearly a hundred years, on a considerable number of subjects. By contrast, attempts to use lucid dreams for therapeutic purposes are clearly still at a very early and exploratory stage.

Whatever may be thought of the ethics and efficacy of releasing your inhibitions by violating social taboos in lucid dreams by, for example, beating up dream figures who irritate you, it is clear that a state which is both realistic and known to be free of real consequences provides an opportunity for experiences which it would be difficult or frightening to obtain in real life. As discussed in Chapter 9 on control of lucid dreams, some subjects have, for example, attempted to repair the deficiencies of their sex lives in lucid dreams, although with varying degrees of reported success. In laboratory experiments it was found that heart-rate increased only moderately during lucid dream orgasm, although in other respects the physiological changes associated with orgasm were similar to those to be expected in waking life (LaBerge, 1985).

Lucid dreams have obvious potentialities in this respect for people who find themselves in isolated or sexually frustrating life situations, though we do not yet know how difficult different types of people may find it to develop this application. If it should prove generally to be the case that the increase in heart-rate associated with dream-sex is only very slight, this might be a useful form of experience for people suffering from heart disease, or who are too ill for some other reason to enjoy normal sex without risks. Furthermore, sex in lucid dreams might have useful applications for some disabled people who would be unable to experience sex in any other way.

People who are unhappy with their actual gender may be able to have the experience of inhabiting a body of the sex which they would prefer to be (see the example from Whiteman, 1961, quoted on p. 74). Similarly, a person who was nervous of public speaking might perhaps gain some benefit from rehearsing his or her situation in a lucid dream. Professor Tholey (Tholey and Utecht, 1987) reports beneficial results for sportsmen and women who rehearse complicated perceptual-motor skills in lucid dreams.

Again, people with physical disabilities are able to experience restoration to normality in lucid dreams. For example, as mentioned in Chapter 4, the French psychologist Yves Delage, who was partially blind, reported pre-lucid dreams in which his sight was restored. This is a possibility which might be developed to the benefit of the disabled, who might find experiences of free functioning and activity in lucid dreams a welcome enrichment of their lives.

Although lucid dreams may have various therapeutic applications of this kind, it is questionable whether they are a particularly efficacious road to the unconscious as some have claimed. Let us consider how this idea may have originated.

Ordinary dreams are commonly supposed to reflect the problems of a person's waking life. Both Jungian and Freudian analysts have an extensive repertoire of symbolic interpretations which are supposed to permit them to translate the message of dreams and gain insight into what they are saying about the dreamer's view of his life situation. It is generally supposed that the dreamer's life problems, as presented by his dreams, include psychological elements of which he is not consciously aware.

In other words, the therapeutic use of ordinary dreams depends on the idea that, by analysing what the dreams represent, the dreamer can be led to a greater insight into the workings of his own psychology, since in this form dreams present him with a more exact version of what he really thinks of his situation, even if not of what is actually the case. Those people who advocate the use of lucid dreams for solving psychological problems therefore tend to assume that the lucid dream provides an equally, if not more, direct access to the unconscious mind. In their view, lucid dream situations present dreamers with opportunities for learning about, and even modifying, their unconscious beliefs and wishes. By interacting in one way rather than another with certain elements of the lucid dream, the dreamer will actually produce an effect on those unconscious parts of his or her own psychology which those particular elements supposedly represent. So, for example, it has been supposed that if a person having a lucid dream meets an ogre which is supposed to symbolise his own less acceptable impulses, and makes friendly gestures towards it, this will not only symbolise but actually bring about an acceptance by the conscious personality of these previously unacceptable impulses.

As yet there seems to be little beyond the subjective impressions of a relatively small number of people that procedures of this kind in lucid dreams are efficacious. Professor Tholey, for example, has specialised in encouraging his subjects to encounter their problems in lucid dreams in symbolic forms. But while it is possible that a lucid dream may lend itself, under suitable direction, to producing symbolic representations of a subject's psychological problems and preoccupations, it remains a question for research how much his psychological position is improved by encountering his problems in this way.

There has perhaps been a tendency to assume that since the conscious mind is so much more present in a lucid dream than a non-lucid dream, so must the unconscious be, an assumption which, if true, would make lucid dreams a meeting ground *par excellence* of conscious and subconscious. While lucid dreams certainly differ from non-lucid ones in the extent to which the normal personality is consciously present in the situation, with a reasonable degree of control of its normal intellectual faculties, it is questionable whether the subconscious mind is any more present or accessible in the lucid dreaming state than in the ordinary dreaming state. As suggested in Chapter 5 on emotions in lucid dreams, it seems as if in some ways the conscious mind in a lucid dream is protected from the impact of any unpleasant content which the subconscious may contribute. The situation is, so to speak, 'conscious mind friendly'. So there is a distinct possibility that the subconscious mind is in fact less, and not more, accessible in a lucid dream than in a normal one.

This is not to say that attempts to work through psychological problems in lucid dreams may not have some beneficial effects, but research on this subject is at a very exploratory stage. We should be thankful for the enthusiasm which inspires some investigators to further efforts, while at the same time remaining cautious and reluctant to be readily convinced.

LUCID DREAMS AND PHYSICAL HEALING

In addition to claims that people have been able to use lucid dreams for 'psychological healing', using the freedom of experience which lucid dreams give them to integrate their personalities or come to terms with unacceptable events, it has also been suggested that lucid dreams may have potentialities for physical healing, although as yet this is largely speculative (see Gackenback and Bosveld, 1989, for a review).

Part of the rationale for investigating lucid dreams as a possible means of self-healing comes from the evidence that purely psychological factors can influence the body's immune system. For example, as Gackenback and Bosveld point out, some success has been claimed for the use of waking imagery techniques in treating cancer patients. A person may be told, for example, to imagine his or her white blood cells killing the cancer. The evidence in this area is still controversial. There is a relative dearth of well-controlled scientific studies, one factor which has to be controlled for, of course, being the fact that cancer may go into spontaneous remission.

However, should the efficacy of waking imaging techniques become established, it is possible that techniques similar to this may be developed and found to be effective in lucid dreams. Lucid dreaming is a state in which the imagery is often clearer and more realistic than the subject can usually achieve in any other state. It is possible that people might use this form of imagery to 'encourage' their physiological defences against illness, although it is unclear by what mechanism this might be supposed to operate.

Analogously, a person who wishes his or her body to stop bleeding from a wound might try to dream that the dream body is bleeding from a wound in this position and then that the bleeding is reducing and the wound is healing up.

The idea that methods might be found for using conscious intention, combined with lucid dreaming, to assist healing processes may find some support from another source. Isolated and dramatic examples of the effects of hypnosis, as well as reports of the physiological control achieved by yogis, suggest that at least certain individuals may be able to exercise a direct effect on certain normally autonomous physiological processes (see Green, 1976, Chapter 7). For example, it appears to be the case that deep trance hypnotic subjects are sometimes able to exercise an unusual degree of control over some physiological functions. Among other things, some subjects seem able to inhibit allergic reactions, stop bleeding, experience anaesthesia and stimulate the flow of blood to a specified area of the skin. There are also suggestions that yogis, who are perhaps comparable in some respects with hypnotic subjects, are able to control their heart-rate and regulate their metabolism (see, for example, Anand *et al.*, 1961). If such mental exercises could be replicated by a lucid dreamer, it might be found that the lucid dream state was as conducive to the control of physiology as is hypnosis or meditation.

Only about 5–10 per cent of the population are thought capable, with present techniques, of entering the deepest stage of hypnosis, and few people are likely to undertake the arduous training which may lead some yogis to the degree of control described. Lucid dreaming, on the other hand, seems to be far more accessible to a much larger number of people, and it is possible that it may have the same potentialities for physiological control as deep trance hypnosis. However, at present we can only speculate whether imagining procedures for lowering blood pressure during lucid dreaming, for example, might result in real lowered blood pressure.

This field is one in which exploratory research is called for, rather than one in which anything has been definitely established, and we must recognise that as yet there is no particular reason to single out lucid dreams as likely to produce successful results. Although lucid dream imagery may be more realistic than the subject could achieve in the waking state, it has to be admitted that as yet there is little reason to believe that it is likely to have a direct influence on the physiological healing process. Even if it does, there is at present no particular reason to suppose that the effect is more pronounced than might be achieved by direct auto-suggestion in the waking state. A person might, for example, having placed himself as far as possible in a relaxed state, simply repeat to himself: 'The bleeding is stopping and the wound is healing up.'

There is certainly scope for controlled experiments to be carried out to see whether the use of such techniques has any perceptible effect, and whether groups of people using various suggestive or imaging techniques in the waking state show more or fewer signs of achieving results than people using similar techniques within lucid dreams.

CONCLUSION

To sum up, it seems to us that there is as yet little strong evidence that lucid dreams are likely to provide opportunities for the development of techniques for curing illness or having any other beneficial physiological or psychological effect. The idea that they might have seems to arise largely from the idea that lucid dreams provide a particularly potent channel of access to the unconscious mind and to processes in the body which are not normally under conscious control. While it is certainly true that a person in a lucid dream has more access than in a non-lucid dream to his normal intellectual faculties and is able to remember what intentions he would like to implement, it seems to the present writers that there is little indication that the lucid dreamer is in a particularly favourable position to affect his own unconscious attitudes or desires. The lucid dream state appears, in general, to be adapted to providing the conscious mind with experiences of a neutral to pleasant type, and to be relatively insulated from the complications of unconscious memories or conflicts. The idea that imagery may be used in would-be healing processes may certainly be explored, but there may well be states, such as those normally induced by hypnotic or autosuggestive techniques, which may be more favourable to affecting the unconscious than the lucid dream state.

Chapter 14

Two possible effects of lucid dreaming

In this chapter we will consider two possible effects of lucid dreaming which are sometimes mooted as hazards associated with the practice, one in the short term and the other more long term. The more short-term hazard is the possible detrimental effect of lucid dreaming on the normal restorative function of sleep. The second, more long-term, consideration concerns the possible negative effect of habitual lucid dreaming on the subject's attitude to everyday life. We do not know of any evidence that either of the supposed hazards has ever yet been realised; however, a discussion of them will raise a number of interesting theoretical points. In particular, the question of the long-term effects of habitual lucid dreaming will give us the opportunity to discuss the question of whether, and in what ways, the phenomenon may have influenced various philosophical traditions, both eastern and western.

POSSIBLE DETRIMENTAL EFFECTS

The question is sometimes raised, particularly by those who have never experienced lucid dreams, whether lucid dreaming could be harmful, by reason of preventing a person from getting a normal night's rest. It is true that episodes of lucidity seem to represent periods of relative 'arousal' during sleep. This is suggested both by the phenomenological characteristics of lucid dreams as indicated by people's verbal reports and by their electrophysiological accompaniments. It might therefore be feared that a person who had been experiencing prolonged or frequent lucid dreams during the night would feel on waking that he had not slept properly.

Another concern which is sometimes expressed is that the lucid dreamer might wake with a reluctance to return to the business of waking life, and a desire to return to the absorbing interest of the dream state, rather as some people, according to anecdotal evidence, may apparently become 'addicted' to meditation, to the extent that it interferes with their functionality in the everyday business of living.

Lucid dreamers who have commented on these points, however, do not confirm these suppositions. The consensus of opinion among them seems to be that lucid dreaming does not interfere with the recuperative function of sleep, and that a person may indeed wake particularly refreshed and well-rested from a night's sleep which included lucid dreaming. Similarly, with regard to the possibility that lucid dreaming might interfere with waking life, there is little evidence for such a proposition. Some lucid dreamers have in fact commented on the way in which an experience of freedom and control in their dreams left them confronting waking life with more positive attitudes, and others have claimed that the exhilarating experiences possible in lucid dreams, such as, for example, a particularly exciting flight over a glamorous landscape, could leave them emotionally revitalised for several days. One subject comments: 'I customarily wake with a cheerful "afterglow" that carries me through the day' (Gilmore, 1984).

The function of sleep is still not properly understood; there are many competing theories, none of which is definitely established (see Horne, 1988, for a review). However, it is our everyday observation that sleep appears to have a recuperative function, both mentally and physically. It is interesting to consider, therefore, why it should be that having even several different lucid dreams in one night does not seem to leave the dreamer less refreshed than if he had slept and dreamt normally.

There are effectively two types of sleep deprivation. The first is a generalised sort, in which the subject's normal amount of sleep is deliberately reduced by a given proportion over a period of several nights. This type of deprivation results in increased sleepiness during the day, reduced performance at tasks requiring sustained vigilance, and, in extreme cases, psychosis-like symptoms such as hallucinations and paranoid thinking.

The second kind of sleep deprivation consists in being selectively deprived of either REM or *delta* (slow wave) sleep. The latter is the deep, 'dreamless' sleep which predominates during the earlier part of the night, while REM phases are associated with the type of dramatic, narrative mental activity that is normally labelled 'dreaming'.

The first experiments on the selective interruption, and therefore deprivation, of REM sleep suggested that such deprivation might have disturbing psychological effects like those of generalised sleep deprivation. Dement (1960) initially reported that REM deprivation led to signs of anxiety and irritability as well as difficulties in concentration. But later studies only found fatigue, confusion and reduced ability to think clearly, all of which can result from non-REM sleep deprivation. Empson comments:

> In retrospect, it seems that genuine concern on the part of the experimenters was communicated to the subjects to provide a potent source of suggestion that they should suffer symptoms of paranoia and hallucinations, and a cumulative sleep loss over the six days of the experiment combined to provide a fertile ground for the production of these symptoms.
>
> (Empson, 1989, pp. 111–12)

As Empson implies, the effects of selective deprivation of a particular phase of sleep are difficult to separate out from the effects of generalised sleep deprivation, since repeatedly waking someone during the night when their EEG shows the start of, say, a REM phase is naturally liable to affect the total amount of time spent sleeping. However, in addition to the effects we have already mentioned in connection with generalised sleep loss, selective deprivation of either *delta* or REM sleep seems to result in a 'rebound' effect, in which the subject shows increased amounts of whichever phase of sleep he has been selectively deprived of in the first few nights of uninterrupted sleep.

Two separate ways in which lucid dreaming might interfere with the recuperative effect of sleep therefore suggest themselves. First, it is conceivable that large amounts of lucid dreaming might lead to symptoms of sleep loss through *delta*-deprivation if the effect were to increase the proportion of the night spent in REM sleep. However, we are not aware of any evidence to support this idea. Since we spend roughly 20 per cent of our total sleep time in the REM phase, there would appear to be scope for someone to spend about an hour and a half dreaming lucidly out of a normal eight hours' sleep, provided that all his or her REM periods could be 'used up' on lucid dreams and he or she did not need to spend time in non-lucid REM sleep as well. This is a considerable length of time, and it may be doubted whether anyone has so far succeeded in spending such a high proportion of any one night in a lucid state. Until someone does, preferably in a laboratory where their electrophysiological state can be monitored throughout the night, it must remain an open question whether protracted lucid dreaming expands the REM periods relative to the non-REM periods, and if so, what effect, if any, this may have on the subject's electrophysiological pattern on subsequent nights.

The second possibility is that lucidity so alters the character of REM sleep that large amounts of time spent dreaming lucidly might lead to effects similar to sleep loss through selective deprivation of REM sleep. Again, there is as yet no evidence for such a supposition as far as we are aware. As in the case of the first possibility, it seems unlikely that anyone has ever spent a sufficient amount of time in one night dreaming lucidly to even test the possibility. And even if he or she did, we would be inclined to doubt that any such effect would emerge since the electrophysiological properties of lucid dreaming sleep do not seem to differ in any qualitative way from those of non-lucid REM sleep.

LUCID DREAMS AND PHILOSOPHICAL ATTITUDE

The second, more long-term, possible effect of lucid dreaming that is sometimes suggested is that the habitual lucid dreamer might lose interest in the normal concerns of everyday life because of his or her preoccupation with the absorbing internal events of the dream life. We do not ourselves know of anyone to whom this has happened, though of course this does not mean to say that it never has or never will in the future.

One area in which it is possible that habitual, or even occasional, lucid dreaming may have an effect on the dreamer concerns what one may call the subject's philosophical outlook. To understand this possibility we need to consider what philosophical implications lucid dreams may have, and the emotional reactions these implications produce in people.

As we noted at the beginning of this book, there are only

occasional references in western literature to the fact that a person who is dreaming may at times be aware of the fact that he is, with little indication of any recognition that dreams in which this awareness is present were significantly different from dreams in which it is not. There are, however, indications that lucid dreams received a certain amount of recognition in the East as a distinct type of experience, and one which could be cultivated.

It seems possible that the failure to make the necessary distinction between a lucid dream and a non-lucid dream arises in part from a psychological resistance to recognising the uncertain philosophical status of the 'external world' of waking life. In order to preserve our belief in the unquestioned status of the physical world, and of our secure grasp of 'reality', it is perhaps desirable that dreams should be regarded as something as distinctly unreal as possible. If it becomes clear that they can rival the waking world in perceptual precision and clarity, and that the state of a person's mental functioning in a dream can seem to be not much different from that of waking life, we may start to ask ourselves uncomfortable questions about how good a claim to superior reality our waking life actually has.

It is possible that unconscious considerations of this sort may still be inhibiting research in several other areas. Hallucinations, for example, seem a decidedly under-researched topic, and when research is done there is usually a perceptible tendency behind it to relegate hallucinations to the category of the 'unreal' by associating them with mental illness or with some physiological defect, rather than paying attention to what they are actually like as a form of experience and their relationship to ordinary perception.

Whether or not it is the case that lucid dreams have lain for so long unrecognised by western culture on account of their association with questions concerning the nature of reality, it seems that such recognition as they achieved in the East was predominantly driven by precisely this association. That is to say, this recognition generally occurred in connection with religious traditions which explicitly discussed, and even appeared to advocate a belief in, the illusory nature of physical reality. Tibetan Buddhists, for example, appear by the eighth century to have recognised the possibility of carrying waking consciousness into the dream state. They apparently regarded the opportunity provided by lucid dreams for a realisation of the subjective nature of the dream state as useful practice for acquiring a similar insight into the nature of waking life:

> The *yogin* is taught to realize that matter, or form in its dimensional aspects, large or small, and its numerical aspects, of plurality and unity, is entirely subject to one's will, when the mental powers have been efficiently developed by *yoga*. In other words, the *yogin* learns by actual experience, resulting from psychic experimentation, that the character of any dream can be changed or transformed by willing that it shall be. A step further and he learns that form, in the dream-state, and all the multitudinous content of dreams, are merely playthings of mind, and, therefore, as unstable as mirage. A further step leads him to the knowledge that the essential nature of form and of all things perceived by the senses in the waking-state are equally as unreal as their reflexes in the dream-state, both states alike being *sangsaric*. The final step leads to the Great Realization, that nothing within the *Sangsara* is or can be other than unreal like dreams.
>
> (Evans-Wentz, 1935, pp. 221–2)

There are indications that methods for achieving lucid dreaming were also cultivated in some quarters in India at about the same time. In the twelfth century a Spanish Sufi asserted that the ability to control one's thoughts in a dream was highly beneficial, and that this ability should be universally sought (LaBerge, 1985; 1988a).

Discussion of the philosophical possibility that life might in some sense be a dream, or in religious contexts the more or less dogmatic assertion that it is, has of course a long history, even in the West, and may be seen as taking two distinct forms. In the first of these, discussed by Descartes, for example, one considers the hypothesis that the experience one is having during what one takes to be waking life is indistinguishable from the experience one is having during sleep.

Mavromatis (1987) points to evidence that Descartes himself had lucid dreams, and that they may have been influential in the genesis of his philosophy. This evidence comes from a biography, Baillet's *La Vie de Monsieur Descartes* (1901). According to Baillet, in 1619 Descartes experienced a series of three dreams, interrupted by wakings, during which he conceived his 'greatest discovery', namely the idea of the unity of the sciences. From

Baillet's account Descartes was lucid towards the end of the third dream, if only temporarily, because while still asleep and 'wondering whether what he had seen was dream or vision, he not only decided while sleeping that it was a dream, but also interpreted it before sleep left him.' Soon, however, 'doubting whether he dreamt or meditated, he woke up without emotion and continued the interpretation of his dream on the same lines with his eyes open.'

It is unfortunate that this evidence is only second-hand, but as far as we know Descartes left no first-hand account of his own dream life. It is worth noting, however, that there is indirect evidence in the *Meditations* that Descartes may have had pre-lucid dreams, if not fully lucid ones.

> How often, in the still of the night, I have the familiar conviction that I am here, wearing a cloak, sitting by the fire – when really I am undressed and lying in bed! 'But now at any rate I am looking at this paper with wide-awake eyes; the head I am now shaking is not asleep; I put out this hand deliberately and consciously; a sleeping man would have no such distinct experiences.' As though I did not recall having been formerly deceived by just such reflections (*cogitationibus*) during sleep! When I reflect (*cogito*) more carefully on this, I am bewildered; and my very bewilderment confirms the idea of my being asleep.
>
> (Descartes, 1954, p. 62)

The second form of the idea that the whole of life might be in some sense a dream, which seems more characteristically to occur to habitual lucid dreamers, consists in admitting a qualitative distinction between waking life and ordinary dreams, but going on to consider that there may be an equally qualitative distinction between waking consciousness and some 'higher' form of consciousness. The relationship between this supposed higher state of consciousness and normal waking consciousness would be analogous to the relationship between normal waking consciousness and non-lucid dreaming.

This latter form of the idea is contained in a number of mystical traditions. It is possible that some of the exponents of the idea may have had lucid dreams themselves, and that this experience may have contributed to their developing the analogy in waking life. The following statement, based on the traditions of Gnostic

Christianity, may provide an illustration of this second form of the philosophical idea.

Most people live, then, in oblivion – or, in contemporary terms, in unconsciousness. Remaining unaware of their true selves, they have no 'root'. The *Gospel of Truth* describes such existence as a nightmare. They who live in it experience 'terror and confusion and instability and doubt and division', being caught in 'many illusions.' So, according to the passage scholars call the 'nightmare parable' they lived 'as if they were sunk in sleep and found themselves in disturbing dreams. Either [there is] a place from which they are fleeing, or, without strength, they come [from] having chased after others, or they are involved in striking blows, or they are receiving blows themselves, or they have fallen from high places, or they take off into the air though they do not even have wings. Again, sometimes [it is as] if people were murdering them though there is no one even pursuing them, or they themselves are killing their neighbours, for they have been stained with their blood. When those who are going through all these things wake up, they see nothing, they who were in the midst of these disturbances, for they are nothing. Such is the way of those who have cast ignorance aside as sleep, leaving [its works] behind like a dream in the night. . . . This is the way everyone has acted, as though asleep at the time when he was ignorant. And this is the way he has come to knowledge, as if he had awakened.'

(Pagels, 1980, p. 125)

The habitual experience of lucid dreaming seems liable to suggest ideas of this kind to at least certain subjects, or to reinforce such ideas if they have considered them already. Thus, for example, it seems to be very natural for a lucid dreamer to say to him- or herself: 'In a dream when I achieve awareness of my situation, my position is radically transformed. Suppose that waking life is itself a dream, then may it not be that in some analagous way it is possible to achieve awareness of its relation to some different state, and thus find one's position radically altered?'

Some lucid dreamers not only speculate in this way, but associate the postulated state of 'lucid living' with enlightenment or Nirvana, as described in Buddhism, or with other notions of mystical enlightenment in other religious or esoteric systems. An example is Stephen LaBerge, himself an experienced lucid dreamer, who proposes such a hypothesis in his book *Lucid Dreaming* (1985). Whether the hypothesis itself has any validity is of course an issue on which lucid dreaming itself, as an empirical phenomenon, does not bear directly. However, it is worthy of note as a psychological fact that the experience of lucidity in dreams may lead to philosophical reflections of this kind.

One might also add that it may be difficult to sort out the direction of causation when considering the relationship between a person's philosophical attitudes and his or her experience of lucid dreaming. It is possible that a certain sort of detachment about life in general or the status of the external world in particular (a detachment not necessarily measured by any existing questionnaire or easy to formulate in such a way that it could be measured by one) is a favourable factor predisposing to the cultivation of lucidity in dreams. Whatever the nature of the relationship between philosophical attitude and propensity to lucid dreams, we know of no evidence that an interest in lucid dreaming has ever led to the sort of quietism or passivity that reduces a person's functionality in everyday life.

Chapter 15

Lucid dreams, arousal and the right hemisphere

AROUSAL

In this chapter we will attempt to integrate some of the main findings concerning lucid dreams into a theoretical framework of a neurophysiological kind. To do this we will be making use of two main concepts, *arousal* and *hemisphere function*.

Arousal can be defined in a number of different ways, according to the type of measurement involved, for example, physiological or behavioural. Weinman (1981) defines arousal as referring to 'a continuum of behavioural and underlying physiological states which range from total stupor to hypermania.' Implicit in this definition is the first of our theoretical premises, namely that arousal is a continuous rather than an all-or-none variable. In other words, at any given moment one is not simply aroused or non-aroused, awake or asleep, but somewhere on a continuum ranging from deep sleep to manic excitement.

It may also be useful to make explicit a distinction between arousal as a *state* of the organism, and *arousability* as a long-term trait, subject to possibly wide individual differences. Each of us may be thought of as constantly fluctuating over time with regard to our general level of arousal, and Claridge (1967) has suggested that there may be individual differences in the rapidity or slowness with which these changes tend to take place in a given person. He proposes that there are variations from person to person in the strength or efficiency of the homeostatic mechanisms[1] governing arousal in the central nervous system, with people consequently varying on a continuum from extreme stability to extreme lability of arousal. We suggest that spontaneous lucid dreamers tend to be people who incline towards the labile end of this continuum.

As indirect evidence for this proposition it is interesting to consider some results obtained by one of the present writers (McCreery, 1993) in a study of 450 people who reported having had at least one out-of-the-body experience in the course of their lives. They were compared on a number of questionnaire measures with a group of 214 controls who had never had an OBE. We think it is reasonable to expect findings about OBErs to apply to some extent to lucid dreamers in the light of the close relationship between lucid dreams and out-of-the-body experiences which we have argued for in this book. To recapitulate two of the main elements of this relationship: there is, first, the point discussed in Chapter 7, that there are cases which are difficult to place unequivocally in one category rather than the other. Secondly, there is the fact that there is a statistical association between the occurrence of OBEs and lucid dreams in a given group of people. In other words, people who report OBEs tend to report lucid dreams and vice versa (see Irwin, 1988, for a review). This fact was illustrated in McCreery's data: 66 per cent of his OBErs claimed at least one experience of lucidity in a dream, whereas only 48 per cent of the controls did so. Moreover, a further finding was that the more OBEs an OBEr had had, the more likely he or she was to report lucid dreaming. In view of these links between the two kinds of experience, then, we think it is reasonable to extrapolate in a tentative way from the findings of the OBE study mentioned above to individual differences concerning lucid dreamers.

In the present context, possibly the most directly relevant difference that was found concerned the scores of the two groups on the 'Hypomania' scale of Eckblad and Chapman (1986). This scale is designed to measure the putative trait of *hypomanic personality* in normal subjects. Eckblad and Chapman characterise people displaying this trait as 'upbeat, gregarious, confident, and energetic people who sometimes display these attributes to a maladaptive extreme, becoming euphoric, hypersociable, grandiose, and overactive, with occasional episodic hypomanic symptoms.' It was found that OBErs scored significantly higher on this scale than the control subjects.

OBErs also scored significantly higher than controls on scales designed to measure the incidence of other sorts of anomalous perceptual experience, such as the Perceptual Aberration scale of Chapman *et al.* (1978), which deals mainly with disorders of the body image, for example, the temporary feeling that one's hands or feet are unusually far away. This fits with the findings of Jayne Gackenbach (Snyder and Gackenbach, 1988; Gackenbach and Bosveld, 1989) that lucid dreamers are more likely than controls to report unusual sorts of perceptual experience such as hypnagogic imagery. It is also possible to see a link between this proneness to anomalies of perception and the arousability suggested by the Hypomania result. We have proposed in Chapter 8 that the class of OBEs which occur under conditions of extreme stress (high arousal) do so because this extreme stress triggers a sleep reaction in the subject. Furthermore, there is evidence for a link between heightened arousal and other forms of hallucination (see Slade and Bentall, 1988 for a review of this topic).

It is also interesting to consider the measures on which there was no significant difference between the OBErs and controls, or on which the OBErs actually scored lower than their counterparts. There were no significant differences on measures of extraversion, or a trait which may be thought of as to some extent its converse, anxiety in social situations. Nor did OBErs score significantly higher on Eysenck's measure of neuroticism (Eysenck and Eysenck, 1975). The OBErs also scored significantly lower than the controls on a scale of 'physical anhedonia' (Chapman et al., 1976), which purports to measure a long-term deficit in the ability to experience the normal sorts of physical pleasure, suggesting that at least in this respect the OBErs were enjoying life at least as much as the non-OBErs. These results, taken together, suggested that the OBErs were not necessarily any less functional and well-adjusted to life than the controls, despite their proneness to heightened arousal and anomalous perceptual experiences.

If we are correct in suggesting that spontaneous lucid dreamers are people whose arousal level is relatively labile, one finding this might help to explain is the association that has been observed between lucid dreaming and migraine. Irwin (1988), for example, comments that subjects reporting lucidity in dreams were significantly more likely to be migraine sufferers than those who never achieved lucidity. Irwin even suggests that subclinical manifestations of the migraine attack may actually be what triggers lucidity in certain subjects; in other words, they are made aware that they are dreaming 'by a physiological state that is not

sufficiently marked to be perceived as a migraine headache but
that none the less constitutes acute stress during sleep.'

We feel, however, that this proposed explanation of the link
between lucid dreams and migraine, although ingenious, is a
little *ad hoc*. There does not appear to be any evidence to support
it apart from the data it is invoked to explain. We suggest, rather,
that it is the long-term disposition to states of high arousal that is
liable to trigger both migraine attacks and lucidity in dreams.

Professor Oliver Sacks has underlined the importance of
arousal in the description and explanation of migraine. He
regards it as essentially a 'centrencephalic seizure', that is, a
seizure originating in the mid-brain, and played out over a period
of hours or days. He writes:

> It is in the middle range – between the vegetative disturbances
> and the cortical disturbances – that the *essential* features of
> migraine may be found: alterations of conscious level, of
> muscular tonus, of sensory vigilance, etc. We may subsume
> these under a single term: they represent disorders of *arousal*.
> In extremely severe attacks, the degree of arousal occurring in
> the earlier or prodromal stages of the migraine may proceed to
> agitation or even frenzy, while the ensuing stages may be
> marked by a subsidence into lethargy or even stupor.
>
> (Sacks, 1970, p. 127)

Sacks goes so far as to draw an analogy between migraine and
certain forms of psychosis with regard to the fluctuations of
arousal involved in both conditions:

> The sequence of a full-fledged migraine . . . has essentially two
> stages: a stage of excitation or arousal, followed by a
> protracted stage of inhibition or 'dearousal'.
> It is in these terms that we may first perceive the proximity of
> the migraine cycle to that of epilepsy, on the one hand, and to
> the more leisurely cycles of waking and sleep, on the other; the
> prominent affective components of migraines demand
> comparison, more remotely, with the excitatory and inhibitory
> phases of some psychoses.
>
> (Sacks, 1970, p. 31)

Our suggestion, then, is that a constitutional tendency to lability
of arousal in the central nervous system will predispose the
individual both to migraine, considered as a *disorder* of arousal,

and to lucid dreams, viewed as a state of *anomalous* arousal during sleep.

Our second theoretical premise will be that arousal not only has various levels of measurement, notably behavioural and physiological, but also that even within the physiological level of description it is not a unitary concept. For example, EEG measures may be used to define 'cortical' arousal, which concerns the cortex or 'highest' level of the brain. Skin conductance level (SCL), which is an indication of the degree of activity of the sweat glands in the skin, may be used to define 'autonomic' arousal. (The autonomic nervous system consists of those parts of the nervous system that are not normally under voluntary control, but instead are 'a law unto themselves', like the regulation of the heart-beat or activity of the sweat glands.)

Furthermore, we suggest that these different measures of arousal, whether behavioural or electrophysiological, do not necessarily co-vary in a simple linear fashion, i.e. all rising or falling in parallel, but may become more or less dissociated from one another (Claridge and Clark, 1982), so that at a given time a person may be behaviourally inert but cortically aroused, for example.

An illustration of the possibility of dissociation between the different forms of arousal is provided by the condition known as catatonia, which is sometimes displayed by schizophrenic patients. A catatonic person may appear behaviourally inert and unresponsive. He or she may even display a condition known as 'waxy immobility', in which the limbs can be manipulated into any given position by another person, and will remain in that position until moved again. Despite this behavioural inertness, Stevens and Darbyshire (1958) argue that catatonia is in fact a state of extreme arousal. They found that their catatonic subjects became more active, behaviourally, with the administration of amobarbital, a sedative. It was as if their nervous systems were so over-aroused that they had 'seized up' behaviourally, and the effect of the sedative was initially to release this inhibition before finally sending them to sleep in the normal way. They conclude:

> We . . . propose that the term catatonic 'stupor' is a misnomer due to confusion of a psychic state with a behavioral manifestation. The psychic state in catatonic schizophrenia can be described as one of great excitement (i.e., hyperalertness),

whether the behavioral manifestation is one of overactivity or underactivity. The inhibition of activity apparently does not alter the inner seething excitement.

(Stevens and Darbyshire, 1958, p. 106)

REM sleep may be thought of as a dissociated state not unlike catatonia. The subject's electroencephalogram (EEG) suggests that he or she is cortically aroused, at least in comparison with non-REM phases of sleep. There are few large-amplitude slow waves, for example, and in general the EEG more closely resembles that of the waking state. At the same time the subject is behaviourally inert, in fact 'paralysed', in the sense that muscle tone is considerably decreased in comparison with non-REM sleep, and the rapid eye movements tend to be the only evidence of mobility. In fact, because of this combination of decreased muscle tone and increased cortical arousal, REM sleep, as we remarked in Chapter 1, has sometimes been referred to as 'paradoxical' sleep.

We suggest that the lucid dream state is paradoxical in the same way as non-lucid REM dreaming, only more so; in other words, that there is the characteristic REM immobility, but with even greater cortical excitation than in a non-lucid REM dream. A number of different lines of evidence converge towards this conclusion.

First, there is the fact that lucid dreamers characteristically show a higher level of intellectual functionality than in the non-lucid state. Secondly, there is electrophysiological evidence that lucid dreaming represents a state of relatively high cortical arousal during sleep (LaBerge, 1988b). Thirdly, questionnaire studies and anecdotal evidence suggest there may be an association between the spontaneous occurrence of lucid dreams and high arousal during the preceding day (Gackenbach et al., 1983; Green, 1968a). Finally, there is the fact, discussed in Chapter 12, that nightmares are one of the factors liable to trigger spontaneous lucidity in sleep.

On the mobility aspect, it is worth reminding ourselves of the experience of paralysis which occasionally occurs in association with lucid dreams and related phenomena (see Chapter 8). In particular, we have quoted two cases associated with lucid dreaming which included this feature. One is the case quoted on pp. 78–9 in connection with the negative emotional element of claustrophobia which occasionally occurs in connection with lucid dreams. The other is Subject E's account of her technique for waking herself from dreams by covering her eyes and withdrawing her thoughts from it, quoted on pp. 97–8.

Gackenbach and Bosveld (1989) have independently noted that lucid dreaming may represent a state even more 'paradoxical' than non-lucid REM dreaming. They draw attention to a study by Brylowski (1986) in which he reports that the H-reflex was even more depressed in lucid dreams than in non-lucid ones. The H- or Hoffman reflex is produced by stimulating the posterior tibial nerve, which is behind the knee; the response is a contraction of the soleus muscle in the calf, which extends and rotates the foot. The reflex, or more accurately its disappearance, is regarded as a criterion of REM sleep, as it is present to a varying degree in all states of non-REM sleep and wakefulness, whereas it is suppressed during REM sleep. Brylowski found that the H-reflex was more suppressed during lucid REM sleep than during any other stage of sleep or wakefulness, including non-lucid REM sleep.

Brylowski's study involved only a single subject, and thus stands in need of replication. But it suggests that at least in this particular case the lucid dream state was one in which there was an even greater dissociation between muscular and cortical arousal, in this instance because of the unusually extreme depression of motor function.

Claridge (1967) suggests not only that individual differences in the strength of homeostatic mechanisms within the nervous system give rise to variations of arousability from one person to another, but that these same homeostatic mechanisms give rise to individual differences in the extent to which different functional sub-systems within the nervous system, such as the cortical and the autonomic, may show dissociation of arousal. People with relatively inefficient homeostatic mechanisms will be more likely to show the sort of functional dissociation between different sub-systems illustrated by the catatonia example discussed above. We would suggest that lucid dreamers may be people who are relatively liable to show this dissociation of function between different arousal systems. Such a hypothesis would explain the relative facility with which they enter the enhanced REM state which we postulate above is associated with lucidity.

One finding which we think is relevant to this hypothesis

concerns the raised incidence of meditation practices among lucid dreamers. Meditation appears, at least in some of its forms, to be another 'paradoxical' state with regard to arousal. Certain subjects appear to enter a state in which cortical arousal is accompanied by extreme physical relaxation (Das and Gastaut, 1957; Wallace, 1970). Harry Hunt has commented extensively on the phenomenological similarities between meditation and lucid dreaming (Hunt and Ogilvie, 1988). Gackenbach and Bosveld (1989) also report that meditators are more likely to experience lucidity in dreams than non-meditators, and present anecdotal evidence that lucid dreams are more likely to occur in a given subject following days on which he or she meditated than on days when they did not. In fact, they advocate the practice of meditation as a means of facilitating the occurrence of lucid dreams in people who have not yet experienced them.

We suggest that there are individual differences in the facility with which people enter the paradoxical state of low muscular and high cortical arousal characteristic of meditation, and that this explains the persistence with which some people persevere with meditation practices when others do not. A facility for entering such a 'dissociated' state would predispose the individual, we suggest, both to succeeding at meditation and to experiencing spontaneous lucid dreams, thus helping to explain the association between the two phenomena.

It is worth noting that McCreery (1993) found meditation practices to be significantly more prevalent among the 450 OBErs in his OBE study than among the controls. There was also some association between the number of OBEs reported and the likelihood of meditation being practised, in that the more OBEs the subject had had the more likely he or she was to be a regular practitioner of meditation.

The ecsomatic experience appears in many cases to be a para-doxical state in the same sense as lucid dreams and meditation. Subjects characteristically describe their mental state during spontaneous OBEs as one of alertness, although they tend to rate themselves as physically more relaxed than normal (Green, 1968b). A similar finding emerged from an experiment carried out by one of the present writers in which subjects attempted to induce ecsomatic experiences in the laboratory (McCreery, 1993). It was found that people who had previously had OBEs tended to rate themselves as having become more physically relaxed over the course of the experiment, although an EEG measure suggested that they had become more cortically aroused, at least compared with controls who had never had an OBE. While not all the OBErs reported an OBE during the course of the experiment, this result nevertheless suggested that as a group they were people with a tendency to enter a state in which cortical arousal was 'paradoxically' associated with muscular relaxation.

HEMISPHERE FUNCTION

The second element of our proposed theoretical framework for lucid dreaming concerns hemisphere function. Table 15.1 summarises the ways in which the two halves of the brain are believed to differ with respect to the functions for which they are relatively specialised.

The word 'relatively' needs to be stressed here. In any consideration of hemispheric specialisation one has to guard against too simplistic an idea of functional localisation. As Andreassi (1989) puts it: 'In the final analysis, even though each hemisphere has its special functions, the entire brain must work as a unit in the processing of stimuli and the preparation of an optimal response.' Similarly, Springer and Deutsch, after reviewing evidence for hemispheric asymmetries from the widely differing

Table 15.1 Formulation of hemispheric differences as contrasting modes of thought

Left hemisphere	Right hemisphere
Analysis	Synthesis
Serial processing	Parallel processing
Sequencing	Nonsequencing
Propositional	Appositional
Logical	Creative
Preoccupation with particular	Holistic approach
Ideation	Imagery
Concern with familiarity	Concern with novelty
Concern with similarity	Concern with difference

Source: Cutting, 1985

methodologies of electroencephalography, blood flow studies, metabolic scanning and nuclear magnetic resonance, comment: 'Each of the measures . . . points to the involvement of many areas of the brain in even the simplest task. There are asymmetries in activity between the hemispheres, to be sure, but they can be very subtle, a fact that should lead us away from thinking about hemispheric specialisation in overly simple terms' (Springer and Deutsch, 1981, p. 107).

Nevertheless, given these provisos, we think it is legitimate, and may be useful, to speculate on the relationship of lucid dreaming to hemisphere function, both in regard to which hemisphere might be relatively active during the state, and in relation to long-term individual differences in relative activity of the two hemispheres. We suggest (a) that lucid dreaming may be a state in which activity in the right hemisphere (RH) tends to predominate over that in the left hemisphere (LH), and (b) that people with a tendency to spontaneous lucid dreaming may be people with a tendency to relative activation of the right hemisphere. This hypothesis may be seen as invoking Claridge's idea of relative dissociation of function in different arousal systems. The two cerebral hemispheres are anatomically highly distinct, even if, as suggested above, they are normally acting in concert.

On the question of hemisphere asymmetry in the lucid dreaming state, we think there are a number of considerations which suggest that the right hemisphere usually predominates during lucid dreaming. First, there is the nature of lucid dreaming considered as a cognitive 'task'. As indicated in Chapters 4 and 5, a lucid dream seems to us to be much more naturally viewed as a task involving the manipulation of visuo–spatial imagery than as one involving the serial processing of verbal or similar symbols, and the former is an activity which tends to be correlated with greater RH activity. Secondly, there is the remarkable realism achieved by the visual imagery of some lucid dreams. Thirdly, there are the intellectual deficits displayed by some, such as the reading difficulty. Finally, and perhaps more speculatively, there are the extreme positive emotions sometimes displayed, amounting on occasion to 'ecstasy'.

On the level of long-term individual differences, some of the evidence for the proposition that spontaneous lucid dreamers are people with a tendency to relative activation of the right hemisphere is indirect. The first such indirect indication to which we would point is the result of the EEG study carried out by McCreery (1993), which we have already mentioned briefly, in which forty subjects attempted to induce out-of-the-body experiences in a laboratory setting. Twenty of these were people who had had OBEs before in a real-life setting, and twenty were controls who had not. The subjects lay on a garden lounger, with goggles made of half ping-pong balls over their eyes, and listened to a twenty-minute relaxation tape comprising both physical and mental relaxation exercises. Following the relaxation procedure they heard ten minutes of 'pink noise', which may be likened to the sound of surf in the distance, while they tried to imagine floating up to the ceiling of the laboratory and looking down on themselves lying below. During this procedure the subjects' EEG was monitored, using two electrodes placed over the left and right frontal lobes respectively.

From the present point of view the result of greatest interest concerned the measure of arousal in the two hemispheres throughout the experiment, namely the median frequency of the EEG amplitude spectrum.[2] It was found, as predicted, that the twenty OBErs showed a relative activation of the right hemisphere as compared with the left during the sound phase, whereas the two hemispheres of the twenty controls failed to show any significant divergence of arousal at any stage. This was interpreted as indicating (a) that the OBErs were more likely than the controls to have a general tendency to dissociation of arousal in the two hemispheres of the brain, and (b) more specifically that OBErs have a tendency to relative activation of the right hemisphere when compared with the left. In view of the close relationship between OBEs and lucid dreams, we would argue that this finding may be expected to generalise to spontaneous lucid dreamers as a group, including those who have never had an OBE.

A group finding reported by Jayne Gackenbach may also be seen as supporting the present hypothesis. She found that lucid dreamers exceeded controls on tests of 'higher level visuo–spatial performance' (Snyder and Gackenbach, 1988; Gackenbach and Bosveld, 1989). The test consisted of an imagery task that required the mental rotation of three-dimensional objects. At the same time lucid dreamers were found to perform no differently from controls on a simple two-dimensional rotation task, although they did perform better on a complex two-dimensional one. Both the more complex two-dimensional task and the three-dimensional rotation test are activities which would be considered to preferentially involve the use of the right hemisphere.

These superior performances seem to have been confined to female subjects. This last finding is of interest, since males are generally held to be more 'lateralised' than females; in other words, their two hemispheres are supposed to become somewhat more specialised than those of their female counterparts. Men are also usually thought to excel at tasks involving three-dimensional visuo–spatial skills, such as taking a car engine apart and putting it together again, whereas girls are supposed to develop linguistic skills earlier in their development than boys.

It may be that another of Gackenbach's findings is of relevance at this point. She believes that women lucid dreamers display a tendency to 'neuronal androgyny', in that they show a greater degree of brain lateralisation than women who are not lucid dreamers. In other words, their degree of lateralisation is more like that of men. It may be that this peculiarity is interacting in some way with degree of visuo–spatial skill to produce the gender difference with respect to the mental rotation task and lucid dreaming.

The relationships between these different variables, gender, visuo–spatial skill, and individual degree of lateralisation, are likely to be complex. But they seem to point to the idea that a relatively active right hemisphere may be characteristic of lucid dreamers.

The raised incidence of meditation practices among lucid dreamers may be relevant to the RH hypothesis. Meditation practices often seem to be aimed at the suppression of serial, analytical thought, which is usually conceived of as a predominantly left-hemisphere function, and its replacement by passive contemplation of an image, whether external, as in meditation on a candle flame, or internal, in the form of a visual image. Even when the meditation consists of the consideration of a verbal 'mantra', as in 'Transcendental Meditation' (TM), or an intellectual conundrum, such as the Zen 'Koan', the object seems to be the stopping of the normal associative processes.

Fenwick (1987) also argues for the particular involvement of the right hemisphere in meditative states on the grounds that the RH 'limbic system' (parts of the right temporal lobe and certain structures underlying it in 'older' parts of the brain) is particularly implicated in 'ecstatic' experiences, including those occurring in some cases of right temporal lobe epilepsy.

It is possible that the raised incidence of migraine among lucid dreamers is also an indication that they have an enhanced degree of functional dissociation between the hemispheres, since one-sided pain is almost a defining characteristic of this condition. As Rose and Davies (1987) put it: 'A disturbance in one cerebral hemisphere could produce one-sided symptoms and a one-sided headache.' Apart from the one-sided pain, they point out that in some migraine sufferers there can be loss of vision from just one half of the visual field, and 'pins and needles' on only one side of the body.

It is interesting to note that the conclusion we have come to concerning the relative activation of the right hemisphere during lucid dreaming is the direct opposite of that proposed by another writer in considering the question, namely David Cohen. He has put forward the suggestion that lucid dreaming may be associated with a shift to left hemisphere dominance, since there is, he says, 'evidence that self-consciousness and controlled imagery is more the product of the left hemisphere' (Cohen, 1979). In support of this, he points to evidence that lucid dreams occur more frequently in the latter part of the sleep cycle than in the earlier part, and suggests that the right hemisphere predomi-nates more in the early hours of sleep, and the left hemisphere more in the later hours of sleep. LaBerge (1988b) remarks, in support of Cohen's model, that 'left-hemisphere abstract symbolic functions are undoubtedly crucial for lucid dreaming.'

We would not dissent from LaBerge's judgement. We would agree that the intellectual performance of lucid dreamers implies that LH activation may be expected to be greater during lucid than non-lucid dreams. However, for the reasons already given, we believe that RH activation in the lucid state should usually show an even greater increment over that displayed in non-lucid phases. In other words, we believe that lucid dreaming involves enhanced levels of activity in both hemispheres, but also an increase in RH activation relative to LH.

We feel that Cohen's hypothesis of a shift from right to left hemisphere dominance during the course of the night is too speculative at this stage to be used in explaining the tendency for lucid dreams to occur more frequently towards morning. We suggest that our knowledge of the neurophysiology of lucid dreaming is still at such a preliminary stage that there may well be other explanations forthcoming in due course for the finding that lucidity occurs preferentially in later REM periods, assuming this to be a robust finding. REM phases themselves become more frequent and occupy an increasing proportion of sleeping time as the night progresses, and this implies that the physiology of sleep is not constant from beginning to end of the sleep cycle. As more becomes known of the neurophysiology of sleep in general, other factors besides the putative increase in LH arousal may be seen as relevant to the occurrence of lucidity. We should note, incidentally, that even if LH arousal should be found to be relevant to the *triggering* of lucidity, this would still be compatible with the hypothesis that, once established, lucidity is characterised by relative activation of the right hemisphere.

LaBerge has himself carried out an interesting experiment on lateralisation during lucid dreams. It concerned the lateralisation of alpha activity[3] associated with certain mental activities on the part of lucid dreamers. The subjects were instructed to carry out predetermined tasks involving either singing or counting. If the mental operations involved were as similar to the waking ones as lucid dreamers believe them to be, it would be expected that, as in the waking state, alpha activity is inversely related to cerebral activity, and will occur more in the hemisphere being relatively underutilised. This expectation was confirmed (LaBerge and Dement, 1982b).

The fact that the phasic responses of the two hemispheres to the specific tasks were analagous to what they are usually found to be in the waking state (i.e. LH dominant for the arithmetical task and RH dominant for the musical one) seems to us to support the validity of looking for a tonic difference in arousal in the two hemispheres during lucid dreaming of the kind we have been proposing. The occurrence of phasic responses to specific tasks, such as mental arithmetic, in which the LH was temporarily dominant, would of course be quite compatible with a tonic tendency to RH dominance in the lucid state.

SOME GENERAL METHODOLOGICAL AND THEORETICAL CONSIDERATIONS

To conclude this chapter, and the book, we should like to make some general methodological and theoretical points which we consider to be relevant to both past and future research into lucid dreaming.

The first point of general methodology we should like to make is to suggest that when working with lucid dreams, experimenters should publish a typical selection of the verbal reports of their subjects as well as the accompanying electrophysiological data, and if possible should keep all the verbal case reports in a form that is both accessible to other experimenters and can be correlated with the instrumental readings associated with the individual subjects. Inconsistencies in experimental results may arise from differences in methods of identifying lucidity, as well as from the fact that a lucid dream will only retain the characteristics of lucidity as long as awareness of the state is maintained, and this is easily lost, the lucid dream lapsing into an ordinary one. The findings of one study, which had reported an association between lucidity and high levels of alpha activity (Ogilvie et al., 1982), was subsequently reinterpreted in the light of revised criteria of what constituted lucidity in the subjects in question (Ogilvie et al., 1983). In addition to ensuring consistent interpretation of dream-types, a collection of dream report material may also provide observations which could stimulate research on a quantitative basis on the phenomenological characteristics of the lucid dream state.

The second point we would urge is that the differences between lucid and non-lucid dreams be kept in mind when interpreting findings from the former and considering whether they might also apply to the latter. There are a number of advantages in studying lucid dreams from the point of view of sleep research in general: it is possible for the lucid dreamer to deliberately carry out predetermined intentions; the mind of a lucid dreamer seems to be more accessible to a waking experimenter than that of an ordinary dreamer; and a lucid dreamer can communicate to a certain extent with an experimenter from within his dream. Because of these factors, it is in some ways easier to investigate the lucid dream state than to investigate the ordinary dream state. We may of course hope that experimental work on lucid dreams will enable us to shed light upon factors which are crucial to the nature of dreaming as distinct from waking. However, there is a danger that results from experiments conducted on lucid dreams will be taken as applying to dream states in general. We think it is important to maintain the distinction between lucid dreams, pre-lucid dreams, and non-lucid dreams. Although some of the results obtained from experiments with lucid dreams may in fact apply to all types of dream, this should not be simply assumed and can only be ascertained by rigorous experiments applied to all three types of dream.

To illustrate this point we refer again to the study of differential hemispheric activity during singing and counting tasks carried out by Stephen LaBerge. The title of LaBerge and Dement's (1982b) paper refers to 'dreamed singing and counting during REM sleep'. However, the fact that certain activities in a lucid dream have certain EEG accompaniments is no guarantee that the same activities in a non-lucid dream would have the same accompaniments. It cannot be too strongly emphasised that a lucid dream is a separate mental state from an ordinary dream, and using lucid dreamers to carry out required tasks is providing information about lucid dreaming, not necessarily about dreaming. We can now say that there are indications that singing and counting in a lucid dream have the same EEG accompaniments as the same activities when awake. It is a separate question what EEG effects will be shown by a non-lucid dreamer who is dreaming of singing and counting.

At the same time – and this is our third main point – the comparative study of the electrophysiology of lucid and non-lucid dreams seems to offer a particularly fruitful line of enquiry. Indeed, lucid and pre-lucid dreams provide us with a new cognitive and physical state which may be compared and contrasted with 'dreamless' slow-wave sleep, non-lucid dreaming and even normal waking consciousness. We already know a certain amount about the electrophysiological characteristics of the lucid dream state, as indicated in earlier chapters. However, more work needs to be done to establish the specific differences between this state and the ordinary dream state. It is only by comparing the precise characteristics of lucid dreams, pre-lucid dreams, ordinary dreams and the waking state that we will realise the full theoretical implications of lucid dreaming.

Rather than using lucid dreams as a source of EEG data about dreaming in general, we should exploit the fact that there are phenomenological differences of an apparently qualitative kind between the lucid and non-lucid state to look for differences between the EEGs of lucid dreams and ordinary dreams.

In any comparative study of lucid and non-lucid dreams we should remember that some of the most important differences seem to reside in the presence in lucid dreams of a subject's higher intellectual and critical faculties. In considering the electrophysiological findings which are distinctive of lucid dreams, we should therefore recognise that any such differences we find may be those which define the presence or absence of critical awareness and rational cognitive functioning.

Experimental findings which relate to dreams in the REM state should be repeated for lucid dreams in order to ascertain whether or not significant differences appear. We have referred to the ease with which a lucid dream lapses into a non-lucid one, and a number of subjects have described the effort which is necessary to maintain lucidity. These facts, and the extent to which lucid dreamers indulge in critical thinking concerning their environment, suggest that lucid dream periods may be characterised by a relative predominance of higher-frequency EEG activity if compared with non-lucid dream periods.

One area in which we think further work could usefully be carried out lies in the repetition of experiments in which the course of a non-lucid dream has been influenced by some outside stimulus in order to discover whether or not a lucid dream is more readily influenced in this way. Experiments have been carried out on ordinary dreams using light flashes, musical notes and even water spray, the latter apparently provoking dreams about showers of rain (Dement and Wolpert, 1958). Experiments have also been carried out to discover whether non-lucid dreamers showed significant reactions when names which, to them, were emotionally loaded were read out (Berger, 1963). Such experiments could all be repeated to see whether differences occur in the case of lucid dreams. The mind of a lucid dreamer appears to be more alert, and it would be interesting to know whether this means he is more readily affected by external stimuli, and more able to recognise and interpret them, or whether, paradoxically, heightened attention to the dream content results in reduced awareness of genuine sensory stimuli.

An interesting illustration of the possibilities of stimulus incorporation in lucid dreams is provided by a dream recorded by Hervey de Saint-Denys (1867), in which the striking of a clock was not only incorporated into his lucid dream but recognised as an external stimulus from which he deduced that he was lying asleep in Paris, where he was living near a noisy clock, and also inferred (apparently correctly) what the time was and how long he had left for sleeping.

In experiments in which Alan Worsley was the subject it was found that he was able to register mild electric shocks to the forearm during lucid dreams. Worsley administered the shocks to himself by dint of particular sorts of eye movement (Schatzman *et al.*, 1988). Worsley has also registered mild electric shocks to the wrist (in this instance not controlled by him) in a non-lucid REM dream. However, the latter experiment took place in a different laboratory and under different conditions from the first, so the two do not constitute a comparative study of his thresholds for such stimuli. It would in principle be possible to repeat both experiments within a single experimental context and compare the subject's sensitivity to standardised stimuli in lucid REM and non-lucid REM phases.

Another example of a variable which could be further investigated to compare lucid and non-lucid REM physiology is ease or difficulty of arousal. The threshold for waking someone from the REM state compared with that for waking them from non-REM sleep has already been studied in a number of experiments (see Cohen, 1979). This type of investigation should also be repeated in order to discover whether there is any difference in the difficulty of arousing REM sleepers from lucid as compared with non-lucid dreams. A possible complication which has to be taken into account is that some lucid dreamers have developed techniques for waking themselves up by specific procedures within their dream, and it would be necessary to use subjects who had not evolved such techniques or who undertook to refrain from using them to avoid contaminating the result.

CONCLUSION

In conclusion, we would emphasise once again the fact that a lucid dream is different from a non-lucid one, and reiterate the suggestion made at the start of this book that the defining condition should remain that the subject should be *aware that he or she is dreaming*. At the same time we should recognise that in association with this awareness there is present a considerable proportion of the subject's normal personality; he or she is critical and self-aware and may exercise a good many of his or her normal intellectual abilities. Therefore, in making comparisons of the electrophysiological readings associated with lucid and non-lucid dreams, we may hope to find indications of variables which correlate with the presence or absence of critical and rational mental functioning, which is present in lucid dreams but not in non-lucid ones. Pursuing this research offers the prospect of providing valuable insights into the neurophysiology of normal cognitive functioning.[4]

Notes

1 Definition, illustrations and historical background

1 An 'out-of-the-body', or ecsomatic, experience is a type of hallucinatory experience in which the subject seems to him- or herself to be in a position which is not coincident with his or her physical body. This phenomenon is discussed in detail in Chapter 7.

2 Lucid and non-lucid dreams compared

1 Freud believed that in dreams the apparent events, or *manifest* content, concealed the underlying thoughts and wishes, or *latent* content, and that the latter had to be reconstructed from the former to arrive at the true significance of the dream. Freud thought that the subconscious mind of the dreamer employed a number of devices to conceal the latent content of the dream, such as *condensation*, or the compression of a number of ideas into a single dream object, *displacement*, whereby the most significant aspects of a dream's content may appear relatively trivial, and *symbolisation*, or the use of dream objects to represent individual people, ideas, etc., according to a more or less standardised code of associations.

4 Perceptual qualities of lucid dreams

1 A similar example from the same subject will be found in Chapter 5 concerning intellectual functioning in lucid dreams (pp. 45–6).
2 'Hypnagogic' refers to the borderline state one enters on falling asleep, as opposed to 'hypnopompic' which refers to the corresponding borderline state on waking. Imagery in the hypnagogic state can resemble hallucination in degrees of vividness and apparent autonomy (independence of the will of the percipient). For two recent discussions of hypnagogic imagery see McKellar, 1989, and Mavromatis, 1987.

5 Memory, intellect and emotions

1 'Apparitions' are cases in which a hallucinatory figure or object is apparently superimposed on the otherwise normal perception of the environment. See Chapter 6 for a discussion of the relationship of this phenomenon to that of lucid dreaming.

6 Lucid dreams and other hallucinatory experiences

1 This was a recollection within the lucid dream of the assertion by Ouspensky (1960) that one cannot repeat one's own name in a lucid dream without waking up. It appears from this and other accounts that Ouspensky's belief – extrapolated from his own experience – was erroneous.

2 The word metachoric was derived from the two Greek roots: μετα, conveying the idea of change, as in the word 'metamorphosis'; and χωρη, meaning 'a place'. The word in its literal connotations is perhaps most appropriate in the case of out-of-the-body experiences and some waking dreams, in which there is an apparent displacement of the subject's point of view; reasonably appropriate in the case of lucid dreams and false awakenings, in which the subject's viewpoint is seldom that of his or her physical body lying in the bed; and least appropriate in the case of apparitional experiences, in which the subject usually continues to 'see' the world from the normal point of view. However, it proved difficult to find roots which more exactly corresponded to the rather abstract idea of 'replacing the entire perceptual field with a hallucinatory one'. In any case, the word is intended purely as a useful descriptive shorthand for the latter rather cumbrous phrase, and is not meant to carry any particular theoretical implication, such as the idea that an actual displacement (in the physical sense) is taking place in any of these experiences.

3 'Un homme qui a la conviction entière d'une sensation actuellement perçue, alors que nul objet extérieur propre à exciter cette sensation n'est à la portée de ses sens, est dans un état d'hallucination.' [A man who has the complete conviction of a sensation currently being perceived, when there is no appropriate external object within the scope of his senses which could excite such a sensation, is in a state of hallucination.] – Esquirol: 'Sur les illusions des sens chez les aliénés' (1832). Quoted in Keup (1970, p. 114).

8 Paralysis in hallucinatory states

1 For a fuller discussion of the evidence that the subject's movements as perceived by him- or herself during metachoric experiences may on occasion be hallucinated, see Green and McCreery, 1975, Chapter 5 ('The substitution of physical sensation').

12 Lucid dreams and the treatment of nightmares

1 The psychiatric diagnosis of 'borderline personality disorder', used more in the USA than Great Britain, takes its name from the psychoanalytic idea that there are people on the borderline between neurosis and psychosis (madness), i.e. more disturbed than neurotics but still accessible to psychological forms of treament. For a discussion of the concept from the perspective of a clinical and experimental psychologist, see Claridge (1985).

15 Lucid dreams, arousal and the right hemisphere

1 'Homeostatic mechanisms' in the present context means those putative mechanisms in the nervous system tending to bring the opposing forces of excitation and inhibition into a state of optimum equilibrium at any given time.

2 The raw 'brainwave' picked up by an electrode on a subject's scalp at any given moment is in fact an amalgam of fluctuations or 'waves' at a number of different frequencies. Using the mathematical technique of Fourier analysis a computer program can break down this complex raw wave into its component frequencies, and calculate the size (amplitude) of each component wave at a given time. In any given experiment only frequencies within a previously chosen range or 'spectrum' are considered. In the present experiment the range was 1 to 30 cycles a second (1–30 Hertz). If the amplitudes of all the component waves within this range are plotted against their frequencies, with the x-axis representing frequency and the y-axis amplitude, then an 'amplitude spectrum' is produced. The median frequency (M50) of this amplitude spectrum is that frequency which divides the area of this plot in half. If the amplitudes of the 'waves' in the higher frequency bands, alpha (8–13 Hz) and beta (13–30 Hz), increase while those in the lower frequency bands, delta (1–3 Hz) and theta (4–7 Hz), decrease or remain constant, then M50 will rise. Conversely, if the amplitude of the lower frequency waves such as delta increases while alpha and beta frequencies decrease in amplitude or remain constant, then M50 will fall. M50 may be thought of as a ratio measure, indicating the relative power of the upper to lower frequencies in the EEG at any given time.

The different frequency bands of the EEG have the interesting and useful property that they seem to be positively correlated with arousal. That is to say, slow delta waves are characteristic of the 'deepest' stages of sleep, theta waves of the hypnagogic state, alpha of relaxed wakefulness and beta of heightened arousal in the waking state. So the median frequency, which is measuring the varying contributions of the power in these four bands to the total EEG, is a sensitive index of arousal, using information from the entire EEG spectrum, not just from the alpha band, as is commonly done in EEG studies of cerebral activation or arousal.

3   The so-called 'alpha rhythm' in the human EEG consists of minute
     fluctuations of electrical potential at about ten cycles a second. It is
     usually most evident under conditions of relaxed wakefulness and
     tends to be 'blocked', i.e. to disappear, if the subject engages in some
     form of effortful attention such as mental arithmetic. For this reason
     a transient decrease in the amount or amplitude of alpha is often
     taken as an indication of activation in the part of the brain under the
     electrode picking it up.
4   The Institute of Psychophysical Research is a registered charity (no.
     236226), and has an ongoing appeal for funds to further its
     programme of laboratory work on lucid dreaming and related
     phenomena. Anyone wishing to obtain further information about
     this appeal, entitled 'Towards Understanding Perception', is invited
     to contact the Institute's Director, Celia Green, at 118 Banbury Road,
     Oxford OX2 6JU.

Bibliography

Allport, G.W. (1924) Eidetic imagery. *British Journal of Psychology*, 15, 99–120.

Anand, B.K., Chhina, G.S. and Singh, B. (1961) *Indian Journal of Medical Research*, 49, 82–9.

Andreassi, J.L. (1989) *Psychophysiology: Human Behavior and Physiological Response*. Hillsdale, New Jersey: Lawrence Erlbaum Associates.

Ardis J. and McKellar P. (1956) Hypnagogic imagery and mescaline. *Journal of Mental Science*, 102, 22–9.

Arnold-Foster, M. (1921) *Studies in Dreams*. London: Allen & Unwin.

Baillet (1901) *La Vie de Monsieur Descartes*. Paris.

Berger, R.J. (1963) Experimental modification of dream content by meaningful verbal stimuli. *British Journal of Psychiatry*, 109, 722–40.

Blackmore, S.J. (1983) *Beyond the Body: An Investigation of Out-of-the-Body Experiences*. London: Heinemann.

Bleuler, E. (1911) *Dementia Praecox or the Group of Schizophrenias*. Translated by J. Zinkin. New York: International Universities Press, Inc (1950).

Broad, C.D. (1962) *Lectures on Psychical Research*. London: Routledge & Kegan Paul.

Brown, A.E. (1936) Dreams in which the dreamer knows he is asleep. *Journal of Abnormal Psychology*, 31, 59–66.

Brylowski, A. (1986) H-reflex in lucid dreams. *Lucidity Letter*, 5, (1), 116–18.

Brylowski, A. (1990) Nightmares in crisis: clinical applications of lucid dreaming techniques. *Psychiatric Journal of the University of Ottawa*, 15, (2), 79–84.

Chapman, L.J., Chapman, J.P. and Raulin, M.L. (1976) Scales for physical and social anhedonia. *Journal of Abnormal Psychology*, 85, 374–82.

Chapman, L.J., Chapman, J.P. and Raulin, M.L. (1978) Body-image aberration in schizophrenia. *Journal of Abnormal Psychology*, 87, 399–407.

Chodoff, P. (1944) Sleep paralysis with report of two cases. *Journal of Nervous and Mental Disease*, 100, 278–81.

Claridge, G.S. (1967) *Personality and Arousal*. Oxford: Pergamon.

Claridge, G.S. (1985) *Origins of Mental Illness: Temperament, Deviance and Disorder*. Oxford: Basil Blackwell.

Claridge, G.S. and Clark, K.H. (1982) Covariation between two-flash threshold and skin conductance level in first-breakdown schizophrenics: relationships in drug-free patients and effects of treatment. *Psychiatry Research*, 6, 371–80.

Cohen, D.B. (1979) *Sleep and Dreaming: Origins, Nature and Functions*. Oxford: Pergamon.

Cutting, J. (1985) *The Psychology of Schizophrenia*. Edinburgh: Churchill Livingstone.

Das, N.N. and Gastaut, H. (1957) Variations de l'activité électrique du Cerveau, du coeur et des muscles squelettiques au cours de la méditation et de l'extase yogique, in *Conditionnement et Réactivité en Electroencéphalographie*, Supplement No. 6 of *Electroencephalography and Clinical Neurophysiology*, 211–19.

Delage, Y. (1919) *Le Rêve*. Paris: Les Presses Universitaires de France.

Dement, W.C. (1960) The effect of dream deprivation. *Science*, 131, 1705–7.

Dement, W.C. and Wolpert, E.A. (1958) The relation of eye movements, body motility, and external stimuli to dream content. *Journal of Experimental Psychology*, 55, 543–53.

Descartes, R. (1954) *Philosophical Writings*, A. Anscombe and P.T. Geach (eds). London: Nelson.

Eckblad, M. and Chapman, L.J. (1986) Development and validation of a scale for hypomanic personality. *Journal of Abnormal Personality*, 95, 217–33.

Ellis, H. (1911) *The World of Dreams*. London: Constable.

Empson, J. (1989) *Sleep and Dreaming*. London: Faber & Faber.

Evans-Wentz, W.Y. (1935) *Tibetan Yoga and Secret Doctrines*. London: Oxford University Press.

Eysenck, H.J. and Eysenck, S.B.G. (1975) *Manual of the Eysenck Personality Questionnaire*. London: Hodder & Stoughton.

Faraday, A. (1972) *Dream Power*. London: Hodder & Stoughton.

Feinberg, I. (1970) Hallucinations, dreaming and REM sleep. In W. Keup (ed.), *Origins and Mechanisms of Hallucinations*. New York: Plenum.

Fenwick, P. (1984) Some aspects of the physiology of mystical experience. In J. Nicholson and B. Foss (eds), *Psychological Survey*, 4.

Fenwick, P. (1987) Meditation and the EEG. In M.A. West (ed.), *The Psychology of Meditation*. Oxford: Clarendon Press.

Fox, O. (1962) *Astral Projection*. New York: University Books. (First published in London, c 1939.)

Freud, S. (1954) *The Interpretation of Dreams*. Translated by James Strachey. London: Allen and Unwin. (First published in German, 1900.)

Gackenbach, J. (1988) Psychological content of lucid versus non-lucid dreams. In J.I. Gackenbach and S. LaBerge (eds), *Conscious Mind, Sleeping Brain: Perspectives on Lucid Dreaming*. New York: Plenum.

Gackenbach, J. and Bosveld, J. (1989) *Control Your Dreams*. New York: Harper & Row.

Gackenbach, J. and LaBerge, S. (eds) (1988) *Conscious Mind, Sleeping Brain: Perspectives on Lucid Dreaming*. New York: Plenum.

Gackenbach, J., Curren, R. and Cutler, G. (1983) Presleep determinants and postsleep results of lucid dreams versus vivid dreams. *Lucidity Letter*, 2, (2), 4–5.

Galton, F. (1883) *Inquiries into Human Faculty and its Development*. London: Dent.

Garfield, P. (1974) *Creative Dreaming*. New York: Ballantine Books.

Gillespie, G. (1988) Lucid dreams in Tibetan Buddhism. In J.I. Gackenbach and S. LaBerge (eds), *Conscious Mind, Sleeping Brain: Perspectives on Lucid Dreaming*. New York: Plenum.

Gilmore, E. (1984) Remarks by a lucid dreamer. *Lucidity Letter*, 3, 6–7.

Green, C.E. (1968a) *Lucid Dreams*. London: Hamish Hamilton.

Green, C.E. (1968b) *Out-of-the-Body Experiences*. London: Hamish Hamilton.

Green, C.E. (1977) *The Decline and Fall of Science*. London: Hamish Hamilton.

Green, C.E. (1990) Waking dreams and other metachoric experiences. *Psychiatric Journal of the University of Ottawa*, 15, (2), 123–8.

Green, C.E. and McCreery, C. (1975) *Apparitions*. London: Hamish Hamilton.

Gurney, E., Myers, F.W.H. and Podmore, F. (1886) *Phantasms of the Living*. London: Trubner & Co.

Hall, C.S. (1953) *The Meaning of Dreams*. New York: Harper & Row.

Hall, C.S. and Van de Castle, R.L. (1966) *The Content Analysis of Dreams*. New York: Appleton-Century-Crofts.

Hartmann, E. (1975) Dreams and other hallucinations: an approach to the underlying mechanism. In R.K. Siegel and L.J. West (eds), *Hallucinations* (pp. 71–9). New York: Wiley.

Hartmann, E., Russ, D., Van der Kolk, B., Falke, R. and Oldfield, M. (1981) A preliminary study of the personality of the nightmare sufferer: relationship to schizophrenia and creativity? *American Journal of Psychiatry*, 138, 794–7.

Hearne, K.M.T. (1978) *Lucid Dreams: An Electrophysiological and Psychological Study*. Unpublished doctoral dissertation, University of Liverpool.

Hearne, K.M.T. (1981) A 'light-switch' phenomenon in lucid dreams. *Journal of Mental Imagery*, 5, 97–100.

Hearne, K.M.T. (1990) *The Dream Machine: Lucid Dreams and how to Control Them*. Wellingborough, Northamptonshire: The Aquarian Press.

Hervey de Saint-Denys, M.J.L. (1867) *Les Rêves et les Moyens de les Diriger*. Paris: Amyot. Reprinted, 1964, by the Cercle du Livre Précieux, Paris. The page reference in the text is to the 1964 edition. Trans. C. McCreery. English edition: *Dreams and How to Guide Them*, trans. N. Fry. London: Duckworth, 1982.

Horne, J. (1988) *Why We Sleep*. Oxford: Oxford University Press.

Horowitz, M.J. (1975) Hallucinations: an information-processing approach. In R.D. Siegel and L.J. West (eds), *Hallucinations: Behavior, Experience, and Theory*, New York: John Wiley & Sons.

Hunt, H.T. and Ogilvie, R. (1988) Lucid dreams in their natural series: phenomenological and psychophysiological findings in relation to meditative states. In J.I. Gackenbach and S.L. LaBerge (eds), *Conscious Mind, Sleeping Brain: Perspectives on Lucid Dreaming.* New York: Plenum.

Irwin, H.J. (1983) Migraine, out-of-body experiences, and lucid dreams. *Lucidity Letter*, 2, 2–4.

Irwin, H.J. (1985) *Flight of Mind: A Psychological Study of the Out-of-Body Experience.* Metuchen, New Jersey: The Scarecrow Press.

Irwin, H.J. (1988) Out-of-the-body experiences and dream lucidity: empirical perspectives. In J. Gackenbach and S. LaBerge (eds), *Conscious Mind, Sleeping Brain: Perspectives on Lucid Dreaming.* New York: Plenum Press.

Kelzer, K. (1987) *The Sun and the Shadow: My Experiment with Lucid Dreaming.* Virginia Beach, VA, USA: ARE Press.

Keup, W. (1970) (ed.) *Origins and Mechanisms of Hallucinations.* New York: Plenum.

LaBerge, S. (1980) *Lucid Dreaming: An Exploratory Study of Consciousness During Sleep.* Unpublished doctoral dissertation, Stanford University, Stanford, CA, USA.

LaBerge, S. (1985) *Lucid Dreaming.* New York: Ballantine Books.

LaBerge, S. (1988a) Lucid dreaming in western literature. In J.I. Gackenbach and S. LaBerge (eds), *Conscious Mind, Sleeping Brain: Perspectives on Lucid Dreaming.* New York: Plenum.

LaBerge, S. (1988b) The psychophysiology of lucid dreaming. In J.I. Gackenbach and S. LaBerge (eds), *Conscious Mind, Sleeping Brain: Perspectives on Lucid Dreaming.* New York: Plenum.

LaBerge, S. and Dement, W. (1982a) Voluntary control of respiration during REM sleep. *Sleep Research*, 11, 107.

LaBerge, S. and Dement, W. (1982b) Lateralization of alpha activity for dreamed singing and counting during REM sleep. *Psychophysiology*, 19, 331–2.

LaBerge, S., Greenleaf, W. and Kediskerski, B. (1983) Physiological responses to dreamed sexual activity during lucid REM sleep. *Psychophysiology*, 20, 454–5.

LaBerge, S., Levitan, L. and Dement, W. (1986) Lucid dreaming: physiological correlates of consciousness during REM sleep. *Journal of Mind and Behaviour*, 7, 251–8.

LaBerge, S., Levitan, L., Gordon, M. and Dement, W.C. (1983) Physiological characteristics of three types of lucid dream. *Lucidity Letter*, 2, 1.

LaBerge, S., Nagel, L., Dement, W. and Zarcone, V. (1981) Lucid dreaming verified by volitional communication during REM sleep. *Perceptual and Motor Skills*, 52, 727–32.

Leaning, F.E. (1925) An introductory study of hypnagogic phenomena. *Proceedings of the Society for Psychical Research*, 35, 289–409.

Levin, M. (1933) The pathogenesis of narcolepsy: with a consideration of sleep-paralysis and localized sleep. *Journal of Neurology and Psychopathology*, 14, 1–14.

Levin, M. (1957) Premature waking and post-dormitial paralysis. *Journal of Nervous and Mental Disease*, 125, 140–1.

Lischka, A. (1979) *Erlebnisse jenseits der Schwelle: Paranormale Erfahrungen im Wachstand und in luziden Traum, bei Astralprojektionen und auf Seelenreisen*. Schwarzenburg, Schweiz: Ansata-Verlag.

McCreery, C. (1973) *Psychical Phenomena and the Physical World*. London: Hamish Hamilton.

McCreery, C. (1993) *Schizotypy and Out-of-the-Body Experiences*. Unpublished D.Phil. thesis, University of Oxford.

McCreery, C. (1994) Dreams and psychosis: a new look at an old hypothesis. In press.

McKellar, P. (1989) *Abnormal Psychology: Its Experience and Behaviour*. London: Routledge.

Malcolm, N. (1959) *Dreaming*. London: Routledge & Kegan Paul.

Marcot, B.G. (1987) A journal of attempts to induce and work with lucid dreams: Can you kill yourself while lucid? *Lucidity Letter*, 6 (1). Reproduced in *Lucidity* (1991), ed. E. Gebremedhin, published by Lucidity Association, 43 Midland Avenue, Berwyn, PA 19312, USA.

Maslow, A.H. (1962) *Toward a Psychology of Being*. New York: Van Nostrand.

Masson, J.M. (1990) *Against Therapy*. London: Fontana.

Mavromatis, A. (1987) *Hypnagogia: The Unique State of Consciousness Between Wakefulness and Sleep*. London: Routledge & Kegan Paul.

Miller, G.A. (1956) The magical number seven, plus-or-minus two. *Psychological Review*, 63, 81–97.

Moers-Messmer, H. von (1938) Traume mit der gleichzeitigen Erkenntnis des Traumstandes [Dreams with concurrent knowledge of the dream state]. *Archives für Psychologie*, 102, 291–318. (Translated by the present authors.)

Moss, K. (1989) Performing the light-switch task in lucid dreams: a case study. *Journal of Mental Imagery*, 13, 135–7.

Myers, F.W.H. (1887) Automatic writing – III. *Proceedings of the Society for Psychical Research*, 4, Part 11, 209–61.

Ogilvie, R.D., Hunt, H.T., Kushniruck, A. and Newman, J. (1983) Lucid dreams and the arousal continuum. *Sleep Research*, 12, 182.

Ogilvie, R.D., Hunt, H.T., Tyson, P.D., Lucescu, M.L. and Jenkins, D.B. (1982) Lucid dreaming and alpha activity: a preliminary report. *Perceptual and Motor Skills*, 55, 795–808.

Oswald, I. (1959) Experimental studies of rhythm, anxiety and cerebral vigilance. *Journal of Mental Science*, 105, 269.

Oswald, I. (1962) *Sleeping and Waking: Physiology and Psychology*. Amsterdam: Elsevier.

Ouspensky, P. (1960) *A New Model of the Universe*. London: Routledge & Kegan Paul.

Pagels, E. (1980) *The Gnostic Gospels*. London: Weidenfeld & Nicolson.

Parkes, J.D. (1985) *Sleep and its Disorders*. London: W.B. Saunders.

Pavlov, I.P. (1960) *Conditioned Reflexes: An Investigation of the Physiological Activity of the Cerebral Cortex*. New York: Dover Publications. (First published 1927 by Oxford University Press.)

Price, H.H. (1964) A mescaline experience. *Journal of the American Society for Psychical Research*, 58, 3–20.

Price, R. and Cohen, D. (1988) Lucid dream induction: an empirical evaluation. In J.I. Gackenbach and S. LaBerge (eds), *Conscious Mind, Sleeping Brain: Perspectives on Lucid Dreaming*. New York: Plenum.

Rechtschaffen, A. (1978) The single-mindedness and isolation of dreams. *Sleep*, 1, 97–109.

Richardson, A. (1969) *Mental Imagery*. London: Routledge & Kegan Paul.

Risberg, J., Halsey, J.H., Wills, E.L. and Wilson, E.M. (1975) Hemispheric specialization in normal man studied by bilateral measurements of the regional cerebral blood flow: a study with the 133-Xe inhalation technique. *Brain*, 98, 511–24.

Robbins, K.I and McAdam, D.W. (1974) Interhemispheric alpha asymmetry and imagery mode. *Brain and Language*, 1, 189–93.

Robbins, P.R. (1988) *The Psychology of Dreams*. Jefferson, North Carolina, USA: McFarland & Co.

Rose, C. and Davies, P. (1987) *Answers to Migraine*. London: Macdonald.

Russell, B. (1948) *Human Knowledge: Its Scope and Limits*. London: Allen & Unwin.

Sacks, O. (1970) *Migraine*. London: Faber & Faber.

Saltmarsh, H.F. (1925) Letter to the Editor. *Journal of the Society for Psychical Research*, 22, 148.

Schacter, D.L. (1976) The hypnagogic state: a critical review of the literature. *Psychological Bulletin*, 83, 452–81.

Schatzman, M., Worsley, A. and Fenwick, P. (1988) Correspondence during lucid dreams between dreamed and actual events. In J.I. Gackenbach and S. LaBerge (eds), *Conscious Mind, Sleeping Brain: Perspectives on Lucid Dreaming*. New York: Plenum.

Schneck, J.M. (1957) Sleep paralysis: a new evaluation. *Diseases of the Nervous System*, 18, 144–6.

Seafield, F. (1865) *The Literature and Curiosity of Dreams*. London: Chapman and Hall.

Sidgwick, H., Johnson, A., Myers, F.W.H., Podmore, F. and Sidgwick, E.M. (1894) Report on the census of hallucinations. *Proceedings of the Society for Psychical Research*, 10, 25–422.

Slade, P.D. and Bentall, R.P. (1988) *Sensory Deception: A Scientific Analysis of Hallucination*. London: Croom Helm.

Snyder, T.J. and Gackenbach, J.I. (1988) Individual differences associated with lucid dreaming. In J.I. Gackenbach and S. LaBerge (eds), *Conscious Mind, Sleeping Brain: Perspectives on Lucid Dreaming*. New York: Plenum.

Springer, S.P. and Deutsch, G. (1981) *Left Brain, Right Brain*. Revised Edn. New York: W.H. Freeman & Company.

Stevens, J.M. and Darbyshire, A.J. (1958) Shifts along the alert–repose continuum during remission of catatonic 'stupor' with amobarbitol. *Psychosomatic Medicine*, 20, 99–107.

Tart, C.T. (1988) From spontaneous event to lucidity: a review of attempts to consciously control nocturnal dreaming. In J.I. Gackenbach and S. LaBerge (eds), *Conscious Mind, Sleeping Brain: Perspectives on Lucid Dreaming*. New York: Plenum Press.

Tholey, P. (1983) Techniques for inducing and manipulating lucid dreams. *Perceptual and Motor Skills*, 57, 79–90.

Tholey, P. (1988) A model for lucidity training as a means of self-healing and psychological growth. In J.I. Gackenbach and S. LaBerge (eds), *Conscious Mind, Sleeping Brain: Perspectives in Lucid Dreaming*. New York: Plenum.

Tholey, P. and Utecht, K. (1987) *Schöpferisch Träumen: Wie Sie im Schlaf das Leben meistern: Der Klartraum als Lebenshilfe*. Niedernhausen/Ts: Falken-Verlag GMbH.

van Eeden, F. (1913) A study of dreams. *Proceedings of the Society for Psychical Research*, 26, Part 47, 431–61.

Wallace, R.K. (1970) Physiological effects of transcendental meditation. *Science*, 167, 1751–4.

Walter, W. Grey (1960) *The Neurophysiological Aspects of Hallucinations and Illusory Experience*. The Fourteenth Frederic W.H. Myers Memorial Lecture. London: Society for Psychical Research.

Warnock, M. (1976) *Imagination*. London: Faber & Faber.

Weinman, J. (1981) *An Outline of Psychology as Applied to Medicine*. Bristol: John Wright.

West, D.J. (1948) A Mass-Observation questionnaire on hallucinations. *Journal of the Society for Psychical Research*, 34, 187–96.

Whiteman, J.H.M. (1961) *The Mystical Life*. London: Faber & Faber.

Name index

Subject index

Lightning Source UK Ltd.
Milton Keynes UK
UKOW04f0255200614

233740UK00002B/59/P